front cover, original artwork by emma stace darling.
jzabagodighee by emma stace darling

emma stace ©2012
www.emmastacedarling.com

ISBN 978-1-291-04508-6

emma stace darling

jzabagodighee

for my mummy

a strange little creature...
an adorable, hilarious, beautiful darling
the wise white worm of guestling.
they never cut the cord, did they mum?

Emma was born in Sussex, England, in the spring, with a great sense of humour, fortunately. She danced, sang, and played the cello and the piano. It was quite clear from a very early age that the theatre was where she belonged, since she found complete fulfilment in expressing herself in this way. Then she went to a London music academy to study classical singing but, feeling too restrained, she left. Classical acting followed, Emma loved Shakespearean roles most, and Emma worked in television and radio, finding voice-over work great fun. And Emma seemed to be a nautral comic,too. The natural progression was to go into musical theatre, though the reality at that time slightly disappointed her. Emma then started to write her own songs at the piano, immediately feeling very at home in the creative medium, performing her songs widely, and then recording some of her prolific output. But she was reluctant to sign her individual style away at that time. She worked as a model for some time, discovering through this work an empowering method of controlling her mind at will, and finding it a surprisingly useful and enjoyable experience. She began to paint, often inspirational, abstract watercolours, and has now moved onto acrylics, and loves the freedom of expression it gives her. She fled to her lifelong love, Italy, two years ago, to study opera and immediately began working as a dramatic soprano, specializing in the grand operatic roles but also feeling an affinity with the more modern chamber operas, adoring both the music itself and the performing. Meanwhile she was giving recitals internationally with a highly acclaimed British pianist, and became the muse of a wonderful and celebrated English composer, who wrote songs for her, and who tragically passed on a few months ago leaving Emma in turmoil. All of this led her to write and everything began to make more sense. JZABAGODIGHEE is Emma's second collection of poetry, the follow-up to GIRL ON FIRE which was highly acclaimed and which surpassed both her expectations and hopes. She is now working on several diverse projects simultaneously (being a female, and therefore able to multi-task). Emma believes in God absolutely and is pretty serious about chocolate and Ravel too. She still finds time for sitting in Italian churches for hours and hours... slowing down her mind to the scent of roses and incense. And eating ice-cream.

stop. i think i get it.

stop.
for the first time
i sit here and muse
positively
on how i can have missed so much
it would've been so much easier
had i been here
light years before

stop.
i look at your old hands
and pinch my skin
to see if mine
stays wrinkled too
they spring back to shape
and smooth skin so
i still have time

stop.
you thought it was so simple
and it is
so you were right
and i begin to see the light

stop.
i think i get it.

poor pan

imagine being a kitchen pan
the awful pressure, if you can
used so often, bashed unfairly
scrubbed and scratched, and praised so rarely
burnt, abused, and yet expected
to perform, and as directed
every time it's taken out
to boil the pasta or the sprout
i feel for pots, they have it tough
because we humans like to stuff
our faces twice a day or more
so why don't they complain or war?
if i were one day one of them
i *would* be potty, stir up mayhem!
i believe things are *all feeling.*
i would bloody hit the ceiling
if a flame were up my arse
twice daily. it's a fucking farce.

hit my head

i danced and danced until in shock
i hit my head hard on a rock
amazing the liquids a body can take
moreover the liquids the body can make
and all of this red came fast out of me
oh! more and more, it seemed to me
to be like heaven, loss of care?
don't know, because i wasn't there.
but when you full extend your hand
and what you see is falling sand
not bones or nails or ring or flesh
and sides of boats turn into mesh
you know you're into something new
it's not for me, it's all for you
and when i look down at my feet
they're slightly melting, almost meet,
can feel my hip joints really push
and join together in the bush.
they need release and all the stone
that cradles the same word as bone
so now the sun drips down through pink
and just like wax blocks up your sink
it stays on me and molds me old
such sensual sex, i talk, i'm told
it's just a whirl, a dervish thrill
with new direction, all my will
beyond horizon, no man's island
i sure cracked my skull in thailand.
what was odd is coming to
i saw four loves, they were all you.

without your salt

oh, you glittering chiffon, free!
come to me, and rescue me.
i'm stifled inside city-scapes
i love their arches, all their shapes
but i can't breathe without your salt
i can't be me, it's not my fault
they're criticised, my senses' ride
i want the blue, the green inside
i want to drown in ecstasy.
i want to die at sea.

who has control

here she comes now, watch the show:

in white cotton
spinning spinning
whirling round
who has control?
tumbling footfalls
head to toe
around again
and i'm afloat
not anchored, joined
to anywhere
to anything
just circling
that spinning girl
who has control?
caught in her own vertigo
embarrassed by its being so
who has control?

dove, the fabric
very plain
off she goes in twists again...
swooping swooping
like a swallow
not with beauty
more with sorrow
who has control?
a nightmare flow of
never-ending head then toe
sing the song a millionth time
head to foot within a rhyme
empty stomach
sick, sick
can't go on spun tight like this
cut the cord
give me a knife
i
just
want
my life

lolled

i have lolled.
i believe that is the word.
given up too many things upon which i relied
at once
...in for a penny...
and i have collapsed
into *gorgeousness*
floating down ophelia's lake
making something beautiful come
out of nothing at all
(emergency call.)

he's holding underneath my neck
my hair is caught under a cheap ring on his finger
it hurts
but not as much
as no pain hurts
no feeling at all
no life.
they think i can't hear what they're saying
they think i'm a junkie girl
they don't see i'm a victim here
of misadvice
bad doctoring
no care at all
from the caring profession

i hear him saying what he did last night...
i want to say "excuse me dear,
one of us isn't feeling tippety top
the last thing i want is the terrifying graphics
of you n suzy-marie from the fair"
oh now they are injecting me
i'd like to know with what
i can't speak
forming words has now become
too much of an effort
the word 'word' is bouncing deeply
to and fro, all stretched,
on a journey
in slow-mo

ooh it's good whatever they gave me
green and violet are my favourites
real violet not mauve or purple
the colour of the sea witch's necklace band

take me somewhere, my beloved
take me back to the still of our air
i didn't do anything to myself here
i want you to love me, rare. rare.

…

here i am in a sterile zone
my sense of humour is intact
i'm aware
i'm running a commentary
in manner of my idol
on the… can't really call them 'furnishings'
and wondering if it's just the drugs
that makes everyone here
seem utterly stunning to me

i think i'll get up.
can't get up.
who's here to help me… help me to rise
i am alone. i'm paralyzed.
panic pricks me all up inside
i can't get up.

i'm up.

oh, i'm down again
"i've come to be with my girlfriend"
i heard him outside coming in to see me
the joy to feel his face pushed up against mine
God, he's an angel
we kissed and we sighed.
"what happened to me then, honey, what's up?"
"my darling love, you died."

ducky

i once knew an anna maria
who everyone used to call ducky
i thought that this moniker deeply un-flattered
her beauty, was odd and unlucky

you get called whatever they call you
he calls me his 'little racoon'?
she calls me 'pips', he calls me 'queenie'?
(the dish ran away with the spoon...)

we socialised quite a lot really
we went to the flicks and for drinks
we bonded together in winter
oh! she was a hoot, and a minx

then our season was springtime
and we used to go for long walks
we ate pizza slices with red wine
and shared some quite epic girl talks

then it got hotter and sweatier
but granita calmed down the heat
we went to the beach and my life stopped
when first i beheld her webbed feet.

little lamb

please don't go to seed on me
oh! please don't go away
i can't be what i want to be
i need you here to stay

when your colour plays around
and sickness starts to fly
take a look at what you've found
and let the past just lie

i cannot be more than i am
i thought i was enough and more
i'm just a tender little lamb
they watch me come, they gnash and gnaw

i'm owed so much that i have earned
i try hard to stay hopeful too
but the fact is i've been burned
so *write about it*'s what i do

i watch your black, it comes and goes
i hope it's just a phase
i'm getting too thin, selling clothes
my life hangs somewhere in your haze

white dress

white dress, lace sleeved
show no flesh
not one of these
they all wear. leaves.

all over its pattern.
silk lies shy beneath.
i shall firmly feel it happen
not in taffeta nor flash satin.

i shall wear this plain dress when
i'm marrying the church.
i want it now, i wanted it then
i didn't know. and so i stem

from that same sacred scented flower
we all do, we who always swear
and fight, cause harm, abuse our power
but i'll become in just one hour

a child of God
all over again.
i was confirmed, how very odd
the year i was deflowered. nod

from those who held me down
the scream
and took away my dream, my crown.
the gypsophila hairband bound

all died the moment i was born.
and i will wear that very frock
i will never more be torn
and no longer soul forlorn.

white dress lace sleeved
my skin all new again, you see?

even a daisy could not have believed
it could be completely re-conceived

ode to fudge-it airlines
in form of shakespearean sonnet

and then we two, so deep in love, turn round -
don't want to but we have to- on our heels
seems like... what i have sought so long, i've found
within his family yule, how safe it feels.
so, smiling, off we went, through customs first
out come my bras, oh nice, they have a feel...
so two hours later, and my humour cursed,
huge dykes with 'things' and me (so no big deal)
the end. we went to board "you've missed it now"
"we got here hours ago, (badge) 'chardonnay' "
next came the sodding trolley hotel plough
and then they tell us that we'll have to pay!
i ask for some redress, it isn't fair.
she says "you see, the thing is, we don't care"

open sky

walking down
through the beaten town
this maltese road
with a light light load
just me

i see
an old guy
open sky
blue for miles
and aisles and aisles
of blowy brown track
birds eye wine rack
hot today
making my way
fifty times quicker
my world is a flicker
of too too great
or just too late.

this guy comes
much closer and hums
something sounding
ethnic surrounding
my aura, my space
he picks up his pace
and then stops.
and drops
to his knees
and with ease
he says "it's you
so can you do
something to prove to me
statues could move to me
renew my faith
i beg you, now?"

in the dust blizzard
he looked like a wizard
grizzled long beard
and dressed pretty weird

and yet he looked to me to be
in a sun dress, honestly
his way to cope
to mend his hope
for if you have that then
you have everything

he stops and he kneels
i come down from my heels
and eye to eye sighting
i could have dived right in
to those pools of pain
running blood in the rain
i felt him so strong
as i held his gaze long
such pain in my chest
how he needed some rest
but he seemed to see me
half woman half deity
his eyes, his eyes
all lilac and wise!
so i told him to touch
but he couldn't move much
or at all with his right
hand, and little left sight

almost blind
i was all he could find
the wind was so hot
but he was....stop.

sincerely i told him
it's not me, it's Him
your sight is perfect
you are perfect
your hand is healed
run home through the field
do what you've longed to do
all through these years

his eyes dropped out jewels
where were life's rules?
now they were brown
looking up, looking down

this was all new to me
what should i do?
he squeezed my hand tight
two amethysts, right
he just passed me weeping
dancing not creeping.
and i felt like keeping his tale dumb
like sleeping.

but high in the season
you might need a reason
for if you have hope then
you have everything
for if you have hope
then you have everything
for if you have hope
then you have everything

(repeat until you believe it)

if i'm not worth it

and did you see my endless pages
full of squiggles, my confession
and did you read them closely
just file them for another session

did you see i just wear black now
did you look from under your cap
would you treat me differently
if i were curled up in your lap?

oh! i want you, feather soft.
for solely you can and must give,
i need your time, your wisdom
and if i'm not worth it,
i don't want to live.

child no child

i see my face
what might have been
had *i* not been so fast
my reactions criticised through life
saved a vast

stop.

could be without nose or eyes
i could be without skin
(i'm already without skin
and in the worst way,
the worst way...)

i came out spotless
hurt my neck
insurance did my car
when a kid runs out of nowhere
nowhere's where you are.

he ran so fast
he was at play
and i was singing strauss
he got to the pavement safe.
i went into the house.

i've never felt such utter joy
relief can get you high
i saw his mum so happy, breathless
she'd been primed to watch him die.

she smiled at me.
i got straight out.
she held so tight, then slapped her son
he cried, well he was just eleven
two young women, one with child

and one with child
who's now in heaven.

mermaid's aria

roll me over down the beach
help me move in total flow
follow my body arms from low
and let the undulations go
yes keep on till they can't stop
they are set in rhythmic back drop
sand is in my hair and eyes
no care i salt-wash once again
and follow the joy of the dance in the sea
and follow the dance of the sea...
until i just can spin no more.

stop.

but float.
floating in still water
palest bue
playing dead
like you

i'll throw my phone away today
i'll not tell them where i am
that has always been my plan
i'm so wrapped up, involved in tune
and time, grand jetée of the dune
one can't explain if one is closed
to this, the heightened frequency
i just want to make art today
with mind, and soul and all my body
use my wrapping that bit further
than we use it in 3d
i want 4d and then 9 octaves
here it is all over me
wet and dripping salty droplets
cover me from north to south
leave nothing unadorned
with those splash splitting broken chords

roll me over down the beach
and take my clothes off on the way
then observe a real live mermaid
laughing loving lust at play!

bluebell walk I

bluebells with your straw, your green
you have a hole within, no seam
the air goes low to high inside
and condensation white and wide
i look at you straight on with gaps
peripherally, bliss perhaps
an earth of purple, heaven pleasure
there's no more, my father's treasure.
all the walks and being cold,
and in God's trees my name carved bold.

bluebell walk II

when the darling bluebells come
i shall be so ripe and sweet
when it's here, that cornflour sheet
i'll wipe my nose and boot my feet

when the darling bluebells come
i'll want to be alone in green
to realise my snow pink dream
and when they speak know what they mean

when the darling bluebells come
how many trees have 'e' carved out
in tuscany? a score no doubt.
falling in love, what's *that* about...?

lovely desirable attractive intelligent living men

all well dressed
clean pressed
well groomed
perfumed
great looking
and cooking
men are...

gay

good times

we had a party here last night
i've done my christian clear-up game
repenting for a good time's weird
but my dad does it, just the same.
the great thing 'bout aperitif
is doing it at home, it's clever.
what could be a cocktail, olives
crisps and bread goes on forever.
four of us. some beer and wine
(in fact it flowed like down stream rain)
we added pizza, and bruschetta
then there was a stop. refrain
i played at my piano songs,
they held me after, and i cried
we gossiped wildly, it was *great,*
and when they saw downstairs they sighed.
in awe of our small studio,
from the pianos, paintings, to
my iconography collection
holding them in rapture, too.

it lasted well into the night
(it has to be the only way)
i love to entertain, to give.
i cleaned my house with joy today!

terrible realization

roses are red
violets are blue
if i could shoot someone
it wouldn't be you

impossible

i thought of chocolate, may and june
to make me feel more happy
i dressed in red not black today
to make my look more snappy

it didn't work, i failed then
to lift myself from flat.
one thinks "i will be happy when…"
it doesn't work like that

i know i feel strange

i know i feel strange
i don't know how
uneasiness, resistance.
too much housework
too much thinking
gazing out of the window.
i don't eat, my stomach is closed.
i just feel strange.

i know i feel strange
bubble gum emetic
it stretches far though, doesn't it?
reminds me of humans
how we bend and stretch for life
trying to be something just out of reach
or we reach it too soon
or not at all
until it's too late.
gosh, i feel strange

i know i feel strange
i don't know how
i see myself as being ok
i look and see an average woman
i feel fine, i'm fine, i am!
i'm just all ill at ease today
something's coming up perhaps
push along the route to the road
to the round bit in the middle
soft like caramel
maybe that will lighten the load
don't worry about me
i just feel strange

it's sunday...
so it's ok

lady mcvickers

our customer, lady mcvickers
when stood in our shop always bickers...
(high prices, low shelves)
how we all piss ourselves
with her dress always tucked in her knickers

hearth

i look to my right
there's a big strong door
the father of the family i
revere and adore

i look down, table cloth
always straight and plain
never showing off, no need
she never has been vain

i look to my left and i can
feel him love me hard, so very hard
he fillets all my fish and meat
he stays my constant safeguard

look further left there is a whippet,
handsome gorgeous gangly teen
he will have his heart done in by
some unworthy beauty queen

looking forward, straight ahead
and there she is, the family's crown.
she gives herself the hardest time
but she's quite happy with her frown

i look to the kitchen stove and see who's
there, the beauty, no-one's darling
looking after, bossing, shouting
laughing, sometimes snarling

i look to the green double chairs
one is for his great white cast
i could drown right in his words
he's the light, his spark shoots fast

the model is hilarious
three times i spat out sprays of coffee
we just catch each other's eye
and even hard rock turns to toffee

i look behind, the tv's there
the centre piece, the fire
it always makes me crick my neck
and what is on is dire

our room is handmade wood, two singles
we make love though all night long
just like being in a cabin
and we stay awake with song

i long for that big wash machine
the barbecue, the bath
that place has made me homesick
it's my centre piece, my hearth.

white hot

i wonder why i'm punished so
and how so, they won't ever know
and guessing gets them in a bind
its easier to think it's *mind*

there is a finite separation
like the platforms at the station
between the state of being mad
and that of being very sad

i feel so cheated out of life
i guess i have one. and this strife.
there are no zones for buffering
in endless white hot suffering

the mask

and so... and so... it's all just so
you stumbled on it, now you know
the effort she puts in to fight
and how she doesn't sleep at night
but falls exhausted to the floor
at midday for an hour or more
you thought her hair had changed, you press
it's in the vacuum cleaner, yes
it falls out when she's over- tired
tea n ciggies keep her wired
enough to do three poems, painting
songs, arranging, endless waiting
without her keeling slowly over
before those seated smug in clover.
looks a breeze, and so she's done it
reached her goal, well, climbed the summit.
all the jealousy she gets
all stuck in stinky female fish nets
colleagues thinking she's had favours
sugar daddies, wild wand wavers.
but she suffered on the coast.
but she would never moan nor boast
she just saw her goal and did
whatever was needed just to keep things hid.
and it was gruelling and tough
and hospitals had had enough…
and then she fell in love and knew
that she could somehow see it through.
and now you know and all i ask
is keep it in, respect the mask.

not knowing

i never have refused my love
i never will refuse
i know this cos i made a pact
with God and with the muse

i built my life on agony
i hold my life on dreams
and when i wake up in the night
it's laughs he hears, not screams

and i believe in miracles
i live on faith, you see
i cannot do the other way.
not knowing works for me

i was the one in that advert

she closes the drawers with her hips
while her charisma oozes
she does it sexily, with flair
(then lots and lots of bruises)

piece of inch

there was a lot of waiting on
that day like all the rest
sweat on palms and sides of nose,
and boxers in my chest
the door was opening so slow
some speed was present somewhere though
for in that tiny piece of inch
i knew it was a 'no'.

living behind

i pricked my finger on a thorn
it bled in lines all down my arm
i stopped and watched, stifled a yawn
there's comfort in a little harm

examining my regal blood
i noticed blue as well as red
it looked as if it did me good
the crimson song of man misled

a petal fell and sealed itself
right onto sticky life line glue
the white against the flow of health
reminded me somehow of you

and so i went inside to eat
my pathway stained the wooden floor
it must have somehow reached my feet
i washed it off but wanted more

the petal, veined in blood was fine
i took a picture with my mind.
i'd use her at some other time,
that virgin we all live behind...

you get very canny when you lead a double life

and he turned slow into a dear
a shell compared to yesteryear
an old boy who could not recall
the dog's name, not a clue at all.

this gift called life is bittersweet
but mostly bitter, thought his wife

the hospital was lit in white
he could not rest in there at night
but wept as he remembered scent
and songs and pictures, when she went

he had lived through fourscore years
and heard enough through long lobed ears
they needed him to stay with them
he only wanted peace, but then

his life just wouldn't let him go.
they suffered on in red... in stead.

he was so immaculate
the best in leather shoes and belts
and finest cotton shirts, all starch
his suits were custom made, with darts

and seams and hand stitched fine detail.
he had the best silk off the rail
for sock and tie and handkerchief.
and naturally dove-white teeth

and was a proud man all his life
and kept it that way too...

so, post visit to the sterile centre
one more cover-up adventure
when the doctor so had wanted
to meet his daughter, he confronted
this sharp pain, by softly turning
to the face all caring, burning

"well, introduce yourself, my daughter
he's looked after me, you oughta
give him thanks, respect and love,
or have you, by some grace above
stopped talking
for the first time in your life?"

to wake and sing

pretty boy
lying here
gazing at me
lovingly
we are two
we need you
it's all spent
all well meant
wake and sing
giggling
early morning
silly things
six o clock
tick tock
lovers knot
mini-maze. stop.
then you start to
knead my heart
tears will drip
and you might slip
rock me baby
make one maybe
stroke my hair
make me stare
i can't ever look away
perfect angel dancer sway
this is real
i can feel
it getting tighter
shining brighter
we so want
to wear a ring
but we can't buy me
anything.
i am yours,
you are mine
do i want more?

no, not this time.

hard and cold vs soft and warm

stiff and starchy
hate it so, with its different colours
denoting how much fear to attach
to every leaf you have to touch.
i hate coins too, weigh you down,
and soon we won't need
euro shinies,
polos cost the most of one
and often two and more in airports
loathe it all.
it's hard and cold.

i need it too
it's like a drug
and with so many
side effects
far worse than the cash itself...

mentally punching random people
when i can't pay my bills or phone
"but i was robbed
i'm not a loser"
it's the truth
i'm not a user

but who's to rail against this life
this luxury we so bemoan?

i'm happy in my own skin so i
touch myself, my soft, warm home.

"now relax, dear" easy peasy, with a total stranger, in a dodgy suit and halitosis peering into my vagina... complete with a supercilious expression and patronising commands like "pop your things off", "pop forward a bit" and "pop your feet in, that's the ticket"... a lot of *popping* going on... bubble wrap city... i had no idea what he was looking for, or at... for commentary there was not... he might have been watching a dvd of the football inside there while i was wincing, for all i knew (but then i would be wincing if i were at home and he were watching footie on my tv, far less a tv set buried three inches inside my body)... "and while i'm 'popping', what will you be doing, setting me on fire inside? leaving your instruments of torture in there again? curing me instantly? hohoho. with your being silent, how would one know?" i thought *loudly*. he said "this won't hurt (me) at all"... "*arggh!*" "i said it wouldn't hurt, you silly billy!" "i'm sorry" i said. then i thought *hang on. no, that it is the last time i say that. not again. no more. after 24 years of apologising for... being in life-robbing agony, and paying for this (mis)treatment.* "no", i say, "but it *did* hurt. i wasn't reacting like that for fun. i trusted you that it wouldn't hurt but then... it did. my jumping was a normal pain response. i don't have a low pain threshold. i'm tough. it's not a personal failing. *you* have what i have everyday, *then* tell me what you just did to me doesn't hurt. don't look at me over your half moons like that, please. i didn't just fall out of the sky. i am daring to speak, not many do, i am telling you the truth. yes with my legs spread and you in between them. i don't like your manner. i am in pain. and after all, you are a man" *or so i was led to believe...*

no reaction at all. as if i had not uttered.

i had had enough pussyfooting around fragile doctors' egos in case they might be able to help me, when in fact they were useless, uncaring and careless in the uk. i had had enough of saying i feel a bit better when i don't in case they might think i am *imagining it* (cos they must appear infallible) as they did when i was 17, and they failed to find what it was then, right at the start. i am still in recovery from the personal insult. i was just the patient, you see.

warning: when doctors don't immediately know what is the cause of patently real suffering, they try to tell you it's in your mind and give you antidepressants to shut you up (which you take because at that point you still trust them) because they think it will convince everyone that they haven't failed... it is you *who have failed,* the patient in pain*, you are mentally unstable or weak, it's not that they just don't know their stuff, or* *can't be bothered to go that bit further because they care.* beware. *i wish i had known that at 17. the course of my life would have been so different. well, i would have had one, for a start.*

and he *actually* said "ooh, we've got a feisty one here" to his nurse.

i was incensed. last straw. "i'm not a circus pony" i said, "and no, we haven't, that's not being *feisty*, i'm just the one that's been in acute crippling unexplained pain, daily, for 24 years, and watched it ruin every aspect of her life, and lost everything to it - career, confidence, social life, self esteem, money. and hidden it, and fought it, exhausted herself, leading a double life. and one who is tired of being hurt inside by people like you, and insulted, to boot, then told to 'pop' off this, and 'pop' on that. no, not feisty, just *seen it all* and *done it all* a million times. you are just another parody of a doctor. and to you i'm just another hysterical woman. one who would give the devil and all his henchmen a blow job to get her life back." the nurse gave me a look as if to say "well done, you go for it."

then he started to behave better. he poked this. this didn't hurt. he poked that. that did hurt. "right, i think we are ready."

"spit spot, i don't have all day", he called over from his great rich man's walnut desk. i said "look, i am wiping the blood and ky jelly from everywhere you left it." gosh, why do gynaecologists all have great big bulbous alien eyes? and whose husband/ boyfriend/ son would want to be one? "i will then put on my stockings and underwear, then my suit and then my jewellery and my shoes and then i will be with you. and by the way, to remind you, i am paying you for this. not the other way round. you are here to help me, right? this has cost me £275, this fifteen minutes of you and your maryfuckingpoppins gynae examination. well, we both have results. here are yours, you failed."

that's the least of it. the very least, that is nothing. one visit. in search of pain relief to get my life started.

but there *was* an answer. i wasn't mad. they had all, just all 261 of them, failed. i had won. they found out what was wrong with me in italy within twenty minutes of a caring careful painless examination and interview. and it was curable.

he was just anothre one to me. he was number 223. he was just another doctor. and i was just another c**t.

the cord

lost in woods known as 'mine' to me
i leant against an unfamiliar tree
and wondered how i'd gone so astray
and late in my walk, on this particular day.
then when my wellie-boots turned, i found
a yellow bird there, looking up, no sound
wagging its 'come-hither' tail (confound
me, wagtails love fringes, water, spaces
not shady thickets, and hemmed-in places).
it turned and swooped away, coy backward glance,
and so i followed suit, in avian trance.
and flitting onwards, veering left and right,
my baton, brief reverberated flight
conducted me to that sharp relief of light.
and soon i sensed that we were nearing
a sky-light in trees, thank God, a clearing.
as i burst free, it fled, what was what
and why was i led to this particular spot?
i heard *my grandma's* voice, in joy, that sound
and, long mute, spoke nothing profound
a modest welcome note, but then... i knew.
a most comforting wonderful thing, or two
that i was free, i'd been found forever
safe, no more lonely nor lost. not ever

gotta run

roses are red
violets are blue
sugar is… *shit!*
i left the iron on

stupid whore

found her in a hotel bar
looking like something from a film
red velvet dress fading
fluff coming off and bare patches, all thinning
smoking as if there were to be a
"don't mind if i do" embargo within minutes.
making every butt, lipstick stained, proof for eternity
that it was you
you did it...
heroine
your lips
your youthful but well travelled hips
you stink of gone off chanel no. 5
it comes out only on high days
not too many, evidently
you are here for an occasion
you are just here to pull focus
to pull him
or to pull something

stupid whore

found drunk on your bed
on your front in stead.
lip pencil dragged down straight as a passage
top to half way down that single bed
over the pale green
eiderdown
pistol still tucked into suspender belt
and yet
you wake up cold with just a splitting head ache
and clots of blood between your splitting arse cheeks

stupid whore

too flattered and drunk to
un-cling those atoms that make a man
a stuttering stoat of a man
with a lick and a click
you missed your trick

stupid whore

it was right before he murdered 6 million jews
and 12 million gentile innocent humans
your fault, you fucking stupid whore

it's a little known fact
but there are lots more

going down

this mind's going down tonight
like the sea climbs down on boats in storm
like rain, it can't go up, it falls
and dries like once wet memory
i can't interrupt the sorrow
it knows where it is needed now
i can only watch and wait
observe and sigh-smile when it leaves
silk parachutes won't rise tonight
they won't obey my will or strength
they only fall and keep on falling
hoping they will land on safe.

this mind's going down tonight
like whisky made him go downstairs
like snow will never shimmy up
and tears will fall down each skin type.

when it hits the lowest ebb
i'll feel like stone, alone and scared
it might be a day, a month
or years, i just won't know right then...
but it will go down, then come up
for nothing's static, we're in motion.
and knowing this will slightly lessen
the terrorising of my little world.

rare

oh the chef in love at work
swooshing noises soon to be edible and quick quick pans...
exquisite objets d'arts will be here soon...
it's the scent of promises kept.

i see my hands over the keys
and see that burn did not go yet
the scar from the car door slam, still there
some people have manicurists,
too much time and money
i have a migraine, is that the same?
but the deep sea noises in our kitchen
cure it calmly
catchy monkey

and hearing him hum from zauberflöte, that boy,
naked but for an apron
the most beautiful male i have ever seen
will approach me soon
and tell me, naked and proud,
lunch is going to be served about now.

we will make love while we eat,
our eyes, our lips, our legs, our toes
i hope that i don't cry or flip
but he would laugh me out of it...

this man is a wisp
but he is immense.
his talent divine.
and he's mine
the savant boy has just begun
and i have seen something so
rare.

this is something rare.

dead man

there once was a dead man from perth
whose corpse was at home, not in earth
he'd not claimed his pension
for too long to mention
and rich maggots mamboed in mirth

but it was

crouching under our walnut table...

i didn't know this would be
part of living the dream.

watching our bed roller skate
around the room
his cleaning up my vomit
while i agonize in my tummy
and our families' hearts all hurt.
it was a night-square
a night-flare
a night where
everything moved.
floors, lamps, books
shelves, pianos, legs
tears, bowels...
bell towers
factories and
ancient regal red buildings.
it was a night of the wrath
of mother nature.
demonstrating
her endless power over us.
i doubt that she laughed though...
her total control over us.
and me?
a speck
no threat to any being at all.

crouching under our walnut table...

i didn't know this would be
part of living the dream.

but it was.

how it happens with me

preface: prince said he wrote music prolifically
so he had something different
to listen to in the car
every day
...i think i write
and paint that way

every day i brush my teeth
i wash my body
choose a scent
normally a green
or myrrh-themed choice
and gently warm up my tired voice
and make sure i won't scare the kids
by putting colour on my face.
put my hair into a plait
sometimes on one side for him...
put dancers clothing on my shape
so i can bend and stretch out, spin
when i want to whisk my air thin.
do it when there is good news
or some music's fall that moves...
or some new flower coming up
or a dove coo like this morning
to accompany the church bells' tune
oh and in bologna too!

then i get my palette out...

i look and stop. and open up
that's all. i open up.

it's quiet inside
he will be sleeping
i see his face and that's enough
to want to make a scene appear
a new one
for God's delight.
it's all for you, you see.

i show him i appreciate
the spectrum of my life
the arcs and arches everywhere

the dips and springs
the running water
sea foam rises up through me
and i shake outside
with or without the seaweed added
and i know it's coming
within a minute or two
it will come, take on a life
complete
all of its own
it goes its own way,
paints itself
takes on its own personality.
and won't go where i want it to.

i want to paint things
and people, too, at times
but He wants *my impression* of it
it seems, he wants my light
so, being as mad as a bag of spiders
it's abstract and it's free.

i can't stop.
two or three poems come
before the pasta's served
i want to stop, and i get wired
but more and more just needs to come
i guess i was blocked up so long
it's all coming out
right now

the muse, she speaks to me in the night:
"the perugino red's not right
it needs less post box and more orange
do it again in the morning light"
she tells me to express myself
whether right or wrong
she tells me to get up at night
and write another song
"another one about school life?"
"another one". she says.
the last one was too 'them', too 'us'
i want it to be 'you' "

this always amazes me
and phases
why would she want to speak through me?
a little runt
a nothing person
pip upon earth.
all feeling, all weaving
"put on your ballet slippers now
and cardy if you're cold
and write about what might have come
if you had been more bold."
and so i write with headphones on
and so i write, make it my own.
record it so it's not all lost
quite quietly, the neighbours cost
me… falling fast at the ivories
and beg her for some sleep now please
she says "alright
but now tomorrow
finish it aloud and sorrow
pain and envy all are gone"
i did it just with slippers on.

and so i rest
but not the muse
so i recite, he says, out loud
sleep talk, but poetry of sorts
but oh! if he would press record...

and sometimes
in a heightened state
or drinking
angst will not abate
it all comes flooding back ...
i sit down and write the
piece that had come to me that
night.

my lover says its funny, breezy
to have a hazy crazy girl
talk verse and rhyme into the air
he smiles and strokes my scented hair:

not rose, or thyme, incense, or lime
but sheer release and turpentine

when

when
it's dark inside
oh! almost black
the air's full flat
a heavy lack,
it's not to stay.
that is to say
her miracles
strike up and play!

when
i needed
one sense, hand feel
could not find
the spinning wheel,
yes one dark time
he bent to say
soft in my ear
to *make* a way

cheers

roses are red
violets are blue
mine's like the roses
a large glass, too

the bomb

and so i touch the night cloth sheets
i look at where my bones shall rest
i do not think that i shall die
i do not think it would be best

i'm wondering what other disaster
is lying before me, joys left behind
i wonder if my friend will make it
or will she softly lose her mind?

today was full of art and music
sorrow, laughter, lightness, cold
sun and moon they wed before me
just before i got too bold

i lie down safely, just for now
times where most are having fun
how hard i gripped through those dark ages
blind, alone, in pain and dumb

and so i touch the night cloth sheets
i look at where my bones shall be
i wonder if the bomb was theirs
or aimed skew-whiff, but meant for me

cloak in november

you're naked in some far off place
trudging through the snow
you are gorgeous, perfect male
your penis hangs down low and heavy
graceful
powerful
your hair is lamp black
and it keeps it all warm down there at the tree trunk
you have no chest hair
but you are not cold.

i made you a pair of fur boots
and covered you in a fur cloak.

took me months to make the cloak,
through july and august
hot to hold the needle, too
slipping all over my naked skin and
stabbing myself
releasing my pain
bleeding over my thigh.
double whammy
so hot, so hot
and you would suck it off and swallow
lick your salty lips
and spit down on mine
my smooth needy petals.
they are yours, too...

and then it was finished,
today you wore it
to protect you well
and you lie on top of me,
naked, freezing but warm in the tunnel
where nobody can find us
not in a zillion icy years
they wouldn't have the first idea
where we stay

or even within which century.
and you lovingly keep me warm
just from the light in your eyes
when you call me your 'queen of fur cloak'.

i just want to be with you
i want to irritate people by worshipping you
i want to annoy women by serving your wishes, none of my own
i want to offend them with the old fashioned adoration
i humbly feel for you, my man.

you are my king.
you are worth my salt, my suffering, my blood.

to be alright

purple wings fall on my shoulders
tickle, rub them with my head
"where're you from, you fey little things
are you spirits, dears?" i said

"when you're dead you're *so* alive
much more than you can ever know
we're in heaven, you're on earth
but we feel you on a dark grey low"

sappho was a grey blue cat
from great siam she hailed
she died when i was just eleven
i thought that i had failed

for if you love and love enough
these things don't come to pass
but then you grow up and you see
a corpse outside, blood on the grass

"i'm just blank, i'll be quite safe
i'll hold him in the night"
the silky mauve thing tells me
it gets easier to be alright.

ghost to rest

you have huge blue curling talons
think you're striking, pale and faint
they're just great big burped up gallons
of your cheap branded gypsy paint…

cross your palms, do your thing, then piss off!
you make me goose hairy, empowered, and wary
i feel your stuff coming up, i need to cough
i can predict, you know, so don't you dare me

you came up here to me, i didn't ask.
found me alone yes, and quite without warning.
i didn't see beneath your human face mask
well, not until that pea fog, dull english morning.

and so now you leave me here, different this time.
trilling the measure, i'm filthy with pleasure
i feel i have put to right that ancient rhyme.
cos i have just stolen *the lot* of your treasure.

hard on

i wonder why
i ask myself
through windows
chin on palm

i think it inside trains
on planes
both whilst in panic
and in calm

i look at paintings then right through them
run the question raw
i do it falling into sleep
and then in slumber, do it more

i toss it endlessly in mind
it's so bad for my health
what made me such a cruel jailor
quite so
hard on
hard on self.

virgin's thigh song

oh woe is me
slick girl, flick city
i run behind in heels, glossy
but can't keep up with them, you see

and the ships roll out
to meet the sky like
cigars from havanna
on a virgin's thigh

oh woe is she
with her baby on her knee
both of them are weeping
and it don't .rain. money

and the ships roll out
to meet the sky like
cigars from havana
on a virgin's thigh

oh woe is he
abused and used so deftly
he's done the same repeatedly
(it didn't count apparently)

and the ships roll out
to meet the sky like
cigars from havanna
on a virgin's thigh   ·

oh woe! for we
who have everything we need!
are so hell bent inventive that
we'll suffer till we're flat-line weed

and the ships roll out
to meet the sky like
cigars from havanna
on a virgin's thigh

would you like to know me, dearest?

"would you like to know me, dearest
would you really, though?
i know you always say you want to
do you truly want to know?

do you want to know where i go
every time i'm gone
i don't think you'd get it, dearest
you don't seem to sing that song...

i will tell you many things
about my life, my love, my mind
but i think at that first hurdle
i would leave you way behind

it's a shame, i love you, dearest
and we work against the clock....
but you think my walking naked
in my own home is a shock."

colour coated peanuts

round...ish
like barbapapa
was it father
or the mother?
is it red
or green
or blue?
will it be
one weird
or two?
feel it
in your fingers now
twirl and curl it
stroke your mouth
stroke your lips
it's not enough
pavlov's dog knows
all this stuff

yes, when they are most fun is when
one's joined to another one

only the good...

walk in front just fragile steps.
leaves behind you, in your wake.
it blows snow to paint those threats.
proof you went for beauty's sake.

a dangerous thing

i am making myself do things today
though every damned thing hurts
or throbs, sweats, oozes, or aches, so, hey,
how can it get much worse?

so i am drinking water here
and eating fennel there
and writing this, a waste of time,
but work combats despair

one feels a sense of "i was here
today, i wasn't dead
i can't have been cos in my fear
i wrote some crap in bed"

a feeling that one saved the day
from landing in the bin.
i'm fevered with a 38
but being idle's sin.

(and is a dangerous thing...)

pure, pure heart

i poured hypnotic potion into your heart
straight from mine
you looked at me.

and looked like purple swirls, turquoise paisley
inside a green and silky room
and you were like a little unicorn, feistily
going for the stars and getting them too.
well you do.
when you do.

i can say no, and send it back, but novices can't and
you're new to the game of human scent swapping.
throw a light ball across the space
and get back bubbles of rainbow to dance in...

look again and roll around,
around like a whirlpool
come again round
and then again over
how happy you are, acute ecstasy!
red rounds, yellow swirls inside their hearts
blowing the wind like weather vanes
and touching my own face
like the one who you love
as if your life depended upon it.

weird is in our game, you mighty beast,
let it in, let it in,
make it normal
to be abnormal,
while getting the strangeness deeper in.
weirdness is in our dance my love.

you are suddenly swimming in clouds
twisting turning thread, snow marshmallows
one wrist of yours is
handcuffed to the candy floss echo
and if it rains?
so we'll catch cold.
a strange cold...

one that makes you feel better than normal.
better then ever.
and weirder than high by the pink sighing skies.
and now we are racing,
really going
swimming up steps that will take us to heaven

and look at you, so calm and relaxed
turning over
looking at me
laughing and seeing the
nonsense of it all.
and nonsense it is.
but also i see
the reality

i do. my darling.
i see someone lovely
punished with a pure, pure heart

my brother I

why must you always dig the knife in?
shove it in-out. then tight-twist it slim.
and sharp the pain, but old the wound.
stick in a zipper sleek silver entombed.
down, up, down again, then take it out
tattoo your initials, as if there were doubt!
don't ever wash it though, just let it fester
laugh at it, afterward, ever the jester.
reds and cranberries, even blacks
worship this joker, you'd best watch your backs.
it hurts like the tale for the thousandth time
she turns her ears *off*, but you sensitize mine
a pain that i'm used to, unlike any other
it shouldn't have been this way. you are my brother.

my brother II

i just caught your face in that picture
the passion blood planted it grows
it's nasty and acid, you rip me up, rhino.
I massively loathe you, as only God knows

you're smug as you're arrogant, über-gauche too
content to withhold your whole ill-gotten lot
and take from us everything, yeah, while you're at it
then stuff every cent in your own bulging pot

so how did you get such a goddess?
deep, talented, sweet millionaire
she loves you (i love you) she'd have to
to stomach the endless "me me" when you're there

you... just got so lucky in *this* life
...were born with these huge golden balls.
people don't like you, but thick-skinned
you screw up your mail, and you censor your calls...

you're spiritually vapid and boast it
and ridicule everyone other
but you'll get a shock at your reckoning day
my beloved shit of a brother

number's lyric

i guess it's just a numbers lyric
how many, how much, the score…
with me it's never nearly enough
i'm constantly desperate for more

winging your fan (for lindsay kemp)

blow into a bubble brave
whiter in glass, power in grace
smokey dancer waft and wave
heavily powdered marceau face

your look is of exaggeration
humour, glamour, horror, choosing
wonder, marvel, exclamation
you spend angel sessions oozing

spend mine wanting you to see
my work again, once more through blue,
thinking how you'd somehow use me...
i'd die, darling, just to fan you

how tough are angels?

saw an angel in my path
and felt i should start creeping
i couldn't rest it was at 4
the whole wide world was sleeping
she said, "i won't go if you run
or sing or make some noise,
we stand still for an earthquake, lion…
stiller still for joy"

dying asleep

and so the symphony and colour dies...
as heavily she pulls my eyes
the lash to kiss the other lash
the light to end the darkness, sash
tied round my whole self loosely now
as sleep will start and slow, oh how
she weeps for one more day gone down
but i am fortunate, a clown
hysterics, when we found that bin
oh how we howled. stop. life, i sin.
and yes i cried, but that's alright
i won't cry any more tonight
i can feel her love today
as gently she relieves my stay

on my shoulder

he's there, gnawing, i hear gnashes
laughing at me sly somehow
post a former billion bashes
aching, hurting, sweating brow

bent over double in pain again
vomiting crying
hopelessly trying
watching people
from the steeple
lead my lovely life
quite free

stopping me from moving on
stopping me from having balance
heavy monkey, heavy con
i can't get past, i can't go on

i feel you but i won't look too
except when i forget and then
in eyelash, i, my mirror, catch you
devil's dare to be there when

i'm 5 times taller even dead
(but-you-have-the-power-cos-you're-in-my-head)
this wired-up withered wilted flower
lived in fear then died in bed

the paths are weird wired
in your favour
whatever it is i'm giving up
will soon have me enslaved again
sad triumph of the words
"i've quit"
are those that make you roar out loudest
closest animal to human,
(that'd make you a right shit)

i feed you bits of human will

and so resent it. i'm so strong.
you've been there, you ugly demon
perching lurching all along
and stealing from me
self-respect
you make me
one more head-fucked insect

you strike hate within me monkey.
but i'm just another junkie.

i built this house on love

i built my house on love, you know
i built my house on love
and everything within this shell
is passed down from above

i built my house on love, you know
i built my house with care
and every cup i chip i'm very
careful to repair

i built my house on love, you know
i painted it with music
it didn't happen in a day
i built it brick by brick

i built my house on love, you know
inside it smells like rose
but why that is, without its presence
nobody quite knows

i built my house on love, you know
i built it for my guest
and only he and i know whom
i worship. now i rest.

liszt

there once was a composer, liszt
who wrote all his stuff stoned and pissed
when questioned about it
he said "never doubt it"
then he and the jounaliszt kissed

the wait I

what am i worth, what am i worth?
waiting to see the bid on me
am i green or blue or red
big horizontal cheque instead
you can't name a price for art
it is what it is, a pounding heart
it's vibrant, sexy, pleasure rife
if it weren't, it would be life.
you can't label me as this
or that, then try to kiss
me, calling me a friend...
i won't kiss back. and i won't bend.
but here i wait. and wait some more
what am i worth? i am a whore.

the wait II

life is just a waiting game
or mine is now, for sure
the mauve waits for the violet
it loves its sister more
the cat is waiting for the mouse
the grey waits for the blue
but this is not like that at all
and is it even true?

the yellow waits for amber
and the labour waits for birth
and debt awaits repayment
so despair, i guess, for mirth
he waits for her, one station and
she waits for him, the other
some, they find themselves in drugs
i wait to find my brother

the crocus waits for springtime
ah, that long wait for the thaw
my red waits for the pain to ease
while fear waits for some more
an endless coma waits for time
to rip the thread apart
they're biding time 'til life can end...
i wait for mine to start

gozo citadel

the majesty of gilt inside
a cooling citadel gozitan built
the figurines, fair floristry
that go with your own gut-felt guilt

i should have walked there often
but only went there for one day
i dreamed of going all year long
i go against my soul, that way

i looked right up, my glasses fell
onto the stone, led me to read
the words that make you hum and hurt
for those beneath, from whom the seed

has passed from one to two to now
and yes their crucifix *does* shock
it's very realistic, felt
my sixth-sense defence quite unblock.

shades down my front, so craning up
raphael, da vinci, michelangelo?
it can't be, in this dot on the map.
there can't be heaven in gozo...

theirs is celestial silence, water
but there is an altar, and there is a rose
they made beauty that we just can't
and how they feel it, nobody knows

citadel you give me joy
you feed me every time i show
you something dark red, heat inside
with need. for what, i still don't know...

tree talk

alone in bluebell forest
i look around to see
if anyone will catch me
while i debut hug a tree

my God! yes, i felt it
i heard its talking too
it told me "i am happy
in all that you will do…

i see the people walking
and hear them making love
no-one knows that which i know
the grail of a lost glove

with great age brings wonder
at what can change in life
you fall for someone, marry them
an empty bed, spoon, fork and knife

they do not believe in magic.
artists have the wherewithal
they feel it, then they give it .
child of mine, i've seen it all

i've seen some ugly suicides,
i too have shed my leaves
i'm sentient, i am all senses
your scent flies upon the breeze

i want your touch your anima
i want you here with me
i only care so much it hurts
come often to your tree"

i will my tree, my father

table for one for eight

there once was a girl in sardinia
who ate for eight, that was just dinn-ier
the meats and the fishes
then dolci, sweet dishes
did not help her fight to get thinn-ier

promises

just like the flutter of a mothling's wing
they pass you, gifting you joyful hope
but then like the skid-flight track dirt dust
off a trucks heel, they are nothing but.... gone
broken bones and faith sorely tested
one questions one's own long-held beliefs.
human beings lie comfy in their skin
and one is alone, singing oh! the same song
you came to me, you flashed my eyes
what was i, a fool to say no?
a jester to laugh at with no intention
of giving me the key to drive on so
i wondered and waited and tried and wept
and nervously tried to encourage it back
i used every page of my positive thought-pack
and never was answered except by a silence
like the sting of a wasp down my throat
the sickening realisation once more.
so your karmic future is looking here bleakly
another one put down to trusting so meekly.
i do not want to be coated in green jade
i will not become lemon-bittered by this
you promised me only a very small thing
and it turned out to be one more butterfly kiss

odd time, lasts about three months, sort of bouncy, all uncoordinated, gangly, involuntarily undulating, yes, bobbing up n down but in air, not water. like a lank monkey, all swinging arms and legs. you can't be king o' the jungle yet! skinny long limbs flopping, flollopping down, and hard fall drop as if they weigh tons. from shoulder to finger a mile the entirety. he's full of life, extremes of expression in a nano-second: japes, grimaces, sudden disproportionate rage. trousers falling down then actually off... because as yet there are no manly buttocks. jerking strangely under enormous ear-hear-music satellite dishes on a girly headband. and that, you see, is 'cool'. we wanted smaller, they want bigger. and that, you see, is 'progress'. kung- fu moves around the kitchen... careful, or that asparagus pie will end up punch kicked through the sky-light, as she shows it off. and there is no night for them... nothing now is new enough, expensive enough, sporty enough, hi-tech enough, no model pretty enough, no car fast enough. he. rules. ice. yet when his special 'friend' - who's not his girlfriend *of course*, of course - sends the wrong text? he'll sob like the big beautiful bubba he is.

gold

there's something sparkling in my vision
peripheral, naturally… twinkling gold
i can't work out what it is or could be though
been over an hour, and i still don't know

my own reflection? in what ? no idea.
my diamond ring's rays hitting the walls?
it isn't responding to movement either…

is it the light that once hit gene kelly
as he sang tap dancing in the rain ?
is it my fairy and her wand recharging
blissfully open to those in the know?

is it my grandmother trying to get through
telling me that funny story's ending?

is it a glow worm? no, not in the day time!
or is it an eye disease as yet unknown?
are they mirrors for vain specks of dust?
is it the inch circus, juggling flames?
is it a big bunch of kids outside playing and
cleverly refracting illuminations?

why just in my right eye and why
when i turn in that same eye still there?

if i were pure i'd know what it were
and be in surest faith, not in fear.
truly one's blessed when the horror is over
for then it's the spirit of God that is here!

tune stalking

the songs i sang go round in sound
they just hang on, they stalk you 'round
steal your mind and get your soul too
by the millionth 'getting to know you'

i *do* know it, i *did* know it...
don't remind me, wretched good bit
then another makes its moaning
like mind-numbing ring-tone phoning

you will kill me if i let you
climb from earth until we reach blue
only panic though surrounded
quite by red, with one more tune dead

when this happens with some strauss
you'd prefer a smurf or mouse
anything to stop crash passion!
something facile and in fashion...

with some putrefying pop song
i can sometimes stray and go wrong
want to bang, hurt, injure self.
they are bad for mental health

but when your own work's on rewind
you'll slow-ly-go deaf and blind
you know it too well, far too sure
just play some tv adverts: cure.

the light in the hall

the light in the hall
reflects the light years
that came and then went
time spilled and not spent
i should have been there
and not here with them all
duty comes
before the fall

move into greens

don't just stop but keep on talking
even though you're out of breath
yours is like the thread of hope there
unseen, strong, to trip an elfin up...
but don't be cruel, you can't be cruel
feel the music lift your wings
and see the trees for what they are
see them sway and then let's pray
pray for continuity...
for rhythm and some form of life
to be uplifted like when he dances
pain and problems, struggle, poverty,
and some laughs for the lucky few
swirling swooping swallowing smoke
that'll melt nicely into wine
purple wants to be with yellow
gold is sick and wants some neutral
beige or blush, or nude or skin
grey just wants to dampen joy
we all wanna be what we are not
you wanted a girl, you got a boy
so when you feel its all just worthless
and the world acts not as it means
watch the elf ho-high jump over
move from blues and into greens

karma honey

i made some blossom honey
i made it just for you
i put my soul straight into it
and perfumed it with dew

the faeries danced around in it
they love the scent of flowers
and i believe these magic dancers
gave it karma's powers

i made it for forgiveness
and saw the benediction through
covered every inch of you
then set the bees free too...

gift tied up

he tied my ankles not with gaffer but with hermes silk
satin tied around my eyes
tongue just tied with anticipation
my knees with chiffon, wrists with ribbon
he had the rest hang down with my hair
my head bent back
my feet just bare

i don't resist
i know who you are
i can smell the back of your neck
and then tar

on the persian rug,
in our italian room
i cannot move
there is no give
i am riding along to the rhythm of trust
desperate, irregular
one learns ones patterns hard
they change you and they test you
like love, like love

i am naked but for stripes of ribbon
there is nothing banal like kink going on
this is french filmic perfection in motion
petals falling fast from the sky like manna,
this is all so spiritual...

i smell burning
no, heat, or something hot
i can smell fire
and then i tighten
a split thrash scalpel nerve
makes my body cook right through
flames and fire freeze-burn this woman
outside, but from deep within

i don't know this smell...
vanilla or hash
exotic or new to me,

caramelise me in my panic
with that thought then
i don't know…
what can i do?
i begin to like the smell
and then want and need it more

you tell me "quite still"
and i am shivering
but it's not cold
not cold at all

then comes what might have been
the last word i hear from you "wait."

what could that mean?

then there is this gap.
this nothing
i feel uneasy, odd inside.
it feels like forever
like i am just spinning
my heart is thumping
questions come in:
how long is nine years to know a person?
no time, if they go quite mad, like you hear…
he could be about to kill me cold blooded
when i was just nearly set for the lad…
a single tear soaks my eye satin
and red silk becomes dark blood from now on….
"why not talk to me, my darling
talk to me?"

"shh"

i wouldn't know how
to speak, any how

and then i hear ravel, the piano concerto, adagio
i love it more than my hands and feet
and feel the fear so harsh so sick
that i can't breathe easily.
stuffed up with sand.

i felt it down there.

something warm spilled down on my front
onto my skin
from a height, i know it well
it's on the side of my forehead too
and it's all dripping down quite heavily
onto my tummy, knees and here
my hair is pulled back from my mouth now
all i hear is
"now say please"
there can't be more !
it's *everywhere.*
he smiles in exhalation, oh
i know that noise
it's a morning thing.
you know that sound
when you can
hear someone smile?

i say "please"
i am no longer afraid
and the joy of the scent begins
to make sense.
he says to use my tongue to taste
but he has it fashioned so i can't quite reach
then mine meets his…

"it's melted and warmed but not too hot
it's 80% chilean cinnamon chocolate
with caramel, just for you
i've had this for nearly two weeks now
and i know that
soon you'll be begging for more"
and then he says
"there's more"

"yes" i think, "there is.
much more.
like love, like love."

fear had made the taste
more sweet, more bitter, more pure
than ever before

piles of books

i closed that book, the pages wet, wet
he is there and i am here
the door's ajar as i wait for signs
i don't know where i am, and i feel nothing

i watch myself as i cream my face
a wild old woman with marbles for eyes
waterproof mascara and a fountain pen
tonight i'll leave the door open wide

then he'll know that i'm here, knowing
he's there knowing. we know, we know
we can't ever be together, and i'm set
to live in roses and piles of books

the horror of the 70s

oh 70s! you led me into life
cherubic gold, pre-raphaelite like child
the sickly psychedelic double knife
it cut the cord, and everything went wild

the grown ups all danced naked round a fire
a woman's pubic hair was more her beard
the decade haute couture snubbed as a liar
and drugs made normal into lumps of weird

and colours looked like luminescent puke
and rhythms felt like fingers half in ears
and chocolate sold like the thin white duke.
and orgies taught us to murder our peers.

maria elena's dinner party

"wow" she said with her 'or' for her 'ow' sound
smoking her 68th ciggy
i ate two plates (it was shop bought)
but tried not to act like a little piggy

she's still just a babe, a bright green 22
but that girl's a charm, she's delightful
with her intuitive art, as a sense
and a humour so pink that it's frightful

i'd forgive anything that could happen
and i so wanna mother her too
i'm here if she needs me, just one thing still jars with me:
burning puff pastry *won't do.*

close enough

look up to the moon
to there from here
here's a circle
there's a sphere

maybe there
they'd understand
the solace of a
'down's' child's hand

the dragging water over grit
her tears
how she fits into it

but no, we just can't 'get' this stuff

when i get sick
i'm close enough

then there's the other big brother nightmare

where isn't there big brother?
where isn't there a cam?
i wonder when i sit and pee
if someone's watching how i am

performing, and Lord knows i hate
the fact that i'm surrounded...
i hate big crowds, i'm claustrophobic
helpless and confounded.

where can i go to be alone?
where can i just be me?
and soon, if not already, camera
circuits will be set in sea...

i don't mind human eyes that pry
that's normal, it's just taking in
all that which is around us.
what i loathe is the not knowing.

i cannot ever be at ease
but i can't change the time
in my bag i have a gun.
soon that won't be a crime

the cups

i wrote on a walk and worried dutifully
if the words would stay with me
i had no pen, no pencil, chalk
and thought "it won't be easy"

i came home well after hours
white rose, a posy in my hand
it was really strange inside
the dainty pastel flowers,
my stone and piece of bark
my band
accompanied my writing
word for word what i'd thought that day
it was quite exciting

i sat on my kitchen chair, hot teas
pressed words like flowers onto the keys

oh God! elating,
excruciating,
to be drinking from both the one cup
and the other cup too!

insomnia inshmomnia

i see it here i see it there
i'm hiding at the kitchen chair
i'll light one up, then i'll be set
but i don't smoke, or i don't yet
deprivation of this kind
will not undo an active mind
it needs to rest, lie with the moon
it needs some help, or i will soon
i light the candle but don't see
what others boast they view clearly
i only see that which appeared
klimt girls kissing, nothing weird
i see it here, i see it there
i'm too wired up to feel despair.
the fall out comes this afternoon
when i will want to die and soon

every sunrise

life is pain.
read that again.
crash position
wait for rain.

big balloon
bursting soon.
one predictable
cartoon.

need to purge
strong the urge.
screaming cats
nerves all surge.

life is pain.
read that again.
every sunrise
smiles in vain.

crocus

oh to get up, dress, and shower
button up my winter coat
then to visualise that flower
put my keys inside my tote

i went outside, post 6 weeks trapped
a blinding sun of lightning
i breathed the air, lungs all but cheered
what they'd been through was frightening

i hear the cafe coffee steam
great buses try to choke us.
and what appears? my very dream!
a peeping-through first crocus

i travel constantly. and i have to say, going through the security check at airports is the most ridiculous malarky these days… you can get through with a needle in your sewing kit in your hand luggage though '*no sharps*' is the rule… you have to take your lipstick out of your make-up bag, annoyingly, and put it in a clear plastic bag (available for 30p, but they're mercifully free at gatwick) because it's 'liquid'… not if it's a lip*stick* it isn't… you can't carry a plastic sinus rinse bottle (costing me £40) because it's "for carrying liquid" "but it has no liquid in it" "well did you wash it after using it" "yes of course" "well then it will still have some liquid in it" … yes and i wore nappies for months 42 years ago, but it doesn't mean i still have poo in my pants now… so i lose my £40 bottle to save my sinuses… my home-made pesto base paste gets confiscated on the grounds that it's liquid, (if you can hold it upside down, as a pate, and nothing pours or leaks, how can it be referred to as liquid?) i tell them to enjoy it with some tagliatelle cos it took me 3 hours to grind the nuts, as a gift for my 94 year old friend lily, with fresh basil from our garden and our own olive oil and parmesan from the very best place in lucca here in tuscany… my 100ml new moschino perfume all wrapped up gets taken away (and trashed, yeah, right) i say "but it's 100ml, that's right", "no, it must be under 100ml" "it IS 100ml or under" "therefore it's got to be 99ml or under" so i say, bewildered, looking at him, softly, "they don't make bottles of 99ml of eau de perfume you strange little moron" "madam, there is no need to abuse me" "yes there *is need*, you need help, clearly, and by my alerting you to that fact, in this calm fashion, it may force you into getting some of same, meanwhile i lose a really emotionally important gift. cheers. it was the first bottle of scent ever bought for me, too, from the man i am going to be with for the rest of my life…"

stupid arses. you have to strip practically naked too. i can't go through the bleep machine, for medical reasons, so i have to stand here taking off my 5 inch heels (a rare occasion usually only seen by my lover in bed) and my coat, my hat, my scarf, my belt, my jacket and my cardigan "want me to take anything else off, or are you just enjoying making me feel totally vulnerable in my stocking feet with my outfit all messed up?" i mutter, as i am standing there, feeling like a vagrant, legs spread like a star fish, my arms wide open as some bull dyke feels under my bra cups to see if they are underwired or not (i am 42 years old and a 36C cup, of course they bloody are…) and then puts her hands up my thighs, very briefly between my legs, over my skirt, down my legs, along my arms, oh yes, all of this in front of everyone… and so it goes on… and i get so fed up with their consistently finding some reason to open my hand luggage… they deflower it every time, my lovingly packed little over-night case, perfection in size and form.

so one day, having had about 85 of these experiences, i finally had had enough and hatched a plan to go on a mission to buy a little something to turn the tables a little, and planted it inside my case, you know, to keep them on their toes. these *little* people with a *little* power are so generous with their smug glances as they say "we're going to have to open this one up i'm afraid, the machine has detected something questionable" (usually a key ring, a watch, or some such threatening or similarly terrifying item) so while my passport, boarding pass, handbag, make up bag, wallet, photos of loved ones, cash, computer etc are all yards and yards away from me and well out of sight, where *anyone* could take them, the fun starts. she opens up my case. she takes out and holds up my suit for tomorrow, leaving it for me to fold up again of course, and everything else, too, my nightie (out in front of her, parallel with her shoulders), my hair piece, and then my bras and knickers, oh yes, not a care in the world for my embarrassment, then she gayly starts doing the same with my tampons, medicines, ky jelly etc… then she picks up something that starts buzzing and *freaks out*. it's long and thick, slightly rocket shaped, over-sized, and has some hand cream carefully coated around the shaft and about 4 inches down too, put there especially for her.

she is red and flushed and sweating a little… i am straight faced and looking on in mock bewilderment as she is actually touching (albeit with gloved hands) "it". but *huge* it is, in veined pink rubber. two pronged at the base (totally revolting. and an expensive way to get revenge, but it had to be done). it is not in any packaging whatsoever. and *everyone* is laughing, not at me , but at *her* as she chases it flying around and buzzing in the air: the guards. the other jobs-worths and passengers are all offered light relief from their own pain. it's no skin off my nose. i am a well dressed woman going off to a meeting in new york, with everything just so, and brimming with confidence these days.

i go up very close to her. "now you know how i feel every time your mates undress me, and feel me up, then you display all my most personal belongings to the whole of heathrow" i say, walk off, case in hand, and have often been applauded .

fede sarda

you are just a ring.
you are not just a ring...

you are golden melted lace
woven, yes, and set apace
you make my hand a better place
for all to see and you to taste.

lick between long fingers mine
and come and worship at the shrine
pin point delicacy pure
neat discretion and its cure
all that was, my love sick pain
i'm not going there again
you are in the other room
we have two, more would be doom
and illness, for we two who long
to be together, joined along
the line in every single track
of breath, and we who always pack
a million kisses in one look.
our story is in solomon's book.

it looks as though it might just bend
or break or bruise but if you lend
a hand to try to change its state
you will fall foul. it's fixed as fate.

stick insect

there once was a stick insects brother
whose jealousy was like none other
the stickiness thing
of his smarter sibling
made him want to shoot, strangle or smother

him.

she's alive

rapid rapid rapid cycle
wash our stuff or feel things change,
feel it moving, don't be scared,
ignore them and their lack of range....
quick, go, act now yes but quickly...
have i lost it, pull those hairs...
sure, so stroke them if it's 'nicer'
am i like a babe upstairs...

you can't tell us you're unbalanced
look how still and calm you look
feel her pulse. no. she's alive, boss
the other one sat and ranted and shook

moods are mainly mine to choose like
chocolate desserts from a squiggly menu
but remember at life's doctor's
it's everybody else in the world, then you.

they do best

to go without, to be without
is not my natural state
but it's happening more and more
18 leanish months to date

i hear it's bravo for the soul
though i was fine with mine
i thought that part of me was set
but i'd been wasting time

when you give up all you want
what you enjoy and relish
it's so weird, but what it does
to your world is embellish

you cherish good, eschew bad stuff
you wonder what you saw in it
roses are godly and beautiful
and they do best too when in shit

God bless the mild (for james taylor)

you have the tunes
they come to you
i don't know how
but they just do

a beatle begged
to have you sing
and so you sang
for him

for us
it seems that every song
is personally through-thought out
hanging in the air and finally falling
onto your guitar
and your one acrylic nail
picks out some love
and then some more
for every piece is full of red
and full of your blue
humble spirit

the women let fast fall down their hair
and sway for you
you look up
when your voice goes down.
in your chords more
beauty than there was before
you came
i think you saw
before

and all distorted.
knew that you were different
graceful parents
thank God for that frozen man
and your darling ma
who saved you from your darker side
at least it saved your life, they tried
and tears can fall as well they might
and you were safe at last, a little
you were safe at night

and rain and fire they drove through you
like my car through that mammoth wall
and out into the world...
your strumming, so right
like you're playing a woman
when you're making love
at night

listen.
what you channel there
is *purity*.
it's from the air
it's not all clever words
and showing off
and me me me me me
with you
it is *real art*
that is to say
"its not for me
it's all for you"

oh gorilla, you rule your kingdom
with the gentle flutter of a mothling wing
a butterfly could not be freer
what you summon up when you sing

you are a wise and sadder man,
you had a bad time in the ban
and it just hurt you,
bubbling your worst enemy
to the upper layers
of your outside state
your skin,
your body
reflected that.
it was for life!
and the Good Lord knows, i understand
mine's for life too, mine is too.
we have to control our monkeys
damn it sometimes.
part of love
i guess

you're seen it all and done it all
so what is left for you now, man?
more beauty, and more beauty still
you're tailor-made for fine maturing
looking ever better
tunes more refined

but the best thing happened there for me
your vocal cords are more in shape
than ever before, in all those years
you sing, such grace
so natural
more sea more night more food more truth
your voice when i heard you in march was finer
than i had even hoped.
how that voice brings doves to tears
and angels walk behind you nodding
like i feel for
theme by tallis,
that same feeling comes to me...
and you make me realise
that age can be so sensual

when i saw an interview from
riding on a railroad
it was like me at my worst, you know?
i felt for you
"stick with the task"
your disdain and pain, your *pain*
was clear as water
from the well,
that of the misfortune
of being an artist

and the glory of it too.

how can i write this then for you?
how do i dare, demi-god, you
i'm an aesthete and obsessed
with anything beautiful at all...
can you be the very best?
never can that be said for sure
but i feel things instinctively
and you play safe,

it works, endures.

and i was so blessed when at college
suffer my first dumb-crash black
i heard one of your albums there
and my life changed. was kinda saved.
i knew that i knew what you knew
i did, too. oh! but, i knew too!
i no longer felt that longing
she who crashed for not belonging

i revere the way you sing
a tune of yours
for the millionth time
as if it were the first
takes my breath.
and how you
show respect for your audience
care for us with
honesty and gratitude.
you sign away
you're never rude
and i'll cheer for you more, and never
tire of your art,
but fade to *forever*

you and yo-yo you make me cry
you and Kim just make me sigh
you n joni's harmonies
are joy in its purest form
they're peace
they are peace.
at last.

what is it you can still want?
i know what i want
what do you?
i want it all, you're surely worth it.
hurt with you, i felt your stuff.

but i suspect that heaven on earth
for your mind would not be enough.

protection

the sea becomes a monster for you
it never will be for me...
i hold a little secret
what you get's not what you see

always been the same

tiny tumbling primroses
turn my hill to cream
dandie-clocks want kids to blow
their green and yellow dream.
i want it for myself you see
i've been quite changed to stone
this freeze is going on and on
i can't do things alone.
i gaze at snow and see a drop
imagine daffodils and rose
the cold has always made me ill
i don't know why, nobody knows.
i shut my eyes and strain to see an
orange flower, unknown name.
i suffer while they have fun
it's always been the same

upon hearing positive news about someone you love

the thrush wing flush-flutters and catches me soft
angels are visibly blown on the breeze
i sit here just sipping and dandelions waft
i prayed for this ending, so God i must please

i plaited my hair, all worn on one side
a ritual easy, to lighten the load
a small random act just to show Him i tried
i kept off all pavements and walked on the road

i wended my way to new places in malta
i stand outside now and i hear one sole insect
i knelt on a prie-dieu and worshipped at altar
i just see it now, hovering in respect

it cannot approach me, i'm circled in gold
the birds are gathered all over the church
i'm happier now, yes, more gracefully bold
(are they in prayer too or famished in search?)

you're just like my family, you're such a love
i don't feel that heaviness, hot in my chest
an aeroplane quietly streaks white above
i know how you tried and i too did my best

the warmth is not searing but massaging joy
i wrote for you daily but hid them from view
the lover, the artist, the boss and the boy
understood only by those dearest few

the lines and the verses were covered in dew
way into night it got cold i was burned
as there on the terrace bells rang, i saw you!
you did it before. then again. now you've learned.

silken thing

little silken blue thing.
fragile fragrant rare.
i want to touch but want you just
to sit still and yes, to stay there.
you tumble over in the breeze.
it's threatening to my relief.
from moods of chain mail heavy pain.
and unseen urgent unsung grief.
i need this flower to pick me up.
i want its silken wing.
i want to fly away again.
and hear my morphine sing.

twisted

it will be a modern vase
sleek-white-straight and desolate
watch it, sterile, clinical,
opposite my chocolate.

up and down it never strays.
then shove nature down its gob.
make it seem like what it's not
and then add water, just the job.

it's all regimented these days.
women's figures, flowers, wood
nothing's curvy, bendy. baby,
i'd be twisted if i could.

petal

a rose petal sits on a pale pale hand
to highlight a dark red smouldering soul
all that she has. her very whole.

a perfect still day. a jailor, she's cruel
why not sigh and let it go?
she seems intent on staying just so

gentle winds come to blow it away
she loved her rose, but nobody knew.
that petal was her dowry. but she lost him too.

tea truffles at night

i laid it on my tongue...
and started to move it
and then began molding it,
tonguing it harder...
it tasted of forests of cocoa dust
also of tea...

well, i guess there's a hole in my glass
cos it's coming out fast
oh!
all over my new top
and in straight lines down my skin
and it's all sticking
onto my flesh;
my breasts and my nipple,
peeling it back off again,
my love...

it leafs off easy
oh God, i feel things like no-one on earth
we *all* say that,
no-one knows if it's true.

burnt my cloud-capped tower on a piece of plaice, you know
while serving his potatoes
there's now't stranger than fact
and you know it
i did it,
you winced for me
it went into blister
but matron or sister
"we were all merry
but mum put on savlon
because of the cord,
you see?"

and he just clips his nails while we're watching the titanic going down
or was it that other big ship? i don't know

i see things in urgency now
i see red
i can't see normally anymore.

he's still here but fading fast right into anima,
we are one, always
the next bit will come.

i know that it's coming,
i know that it's near me,
and i hear that snipping noise so i'm still here.

truffles are good with this mirto, dear xander,
and how your savoy would be proud of me now!

and now he is scraping and
i guess it's normal and
i see my ring on my hand so i'm me.

i spoke to my mother
i emailed my friends
i sense things so strongly
i just can't explain.

air becomes white noise
and sound is distorted
i feel it all coming
it soon will be here. stop.
will there be pain, Lord,
will there be elation,
or nothingness oozing from sterilised pores?

i cannot stand straightness
i only see curves
and when there is factory produce,
my nerves…

i eat your sex, *chocolat*,
all my buds out for you...
they're just in search
of a thrill or a change.
much like a man.
and so, my slick goddaughter,
don't lose your head, holly
when some guy tells you that you are
the one he's been waiting for longingly
all of his life.

he has stopped snipping
and i am still slipping
but things are more cashmere,
mosaics smoothed-out,
and i am still here thank God
yes, i'm still here.

i ate that dark truffle
and then just a couple
to keep it in company...
well just a little.
we all had a tipple
and then had a triple
and now we are here for the night... it is clear.
tomorrow we might have to go to ikea.

oh Christ.

you are poison

breathing in your toxic being
wafting in through me
i am in my golden egg now
you are in my pee

can it be that you are poison?
you are made of ink
can you start to understand
the world would watch you sink?

you can't touch me with your evil
i am in no fear.
i'll just bring a mirror for you.
i am in the clear.

musing on being a chocolate critic

the brown stuff is alive in me
the darker the better these days
the solid, wet, the liquid too
i love it in so many ways

the post arrives and there's a box
beauty, all cardboard and ties
that can really start me going
lust is in my eyes

then the sex starts in my body
ooh and where it reaches.
then i slit the shrink wrap gently
i smell cocoa and peaches

and i let my senses swirl
and open up my womanhood
i get a scent of caramel
then chilli, God it feels so good

i am feeling vaguely rotten
don't know why, free-floating thing
but when i catch a waft of
pecan gianduja i'm gloating

i'm smiling as i start to see
the package as a whole.
i trace the edges of the heart-
shaped box and fill my soul

i wouldn't dream of putting one
onto my loving tongue
not for days or even a week
until this part of my job is done

to touch the chocolate truffles shape
and stroke it like a phallus
it's more like reverence to me
it's holy, it's my chalice

i mean that with sincerity
and if you doubt, you're wrong
i touch them for some minutes
sometimes talking to them long

i look i smell i touch i bite
the last one comes far down the line
and then i feel the textured
back of my front teeth and start to dine

i need to feel the smoothness
if it's granular or gritty, not
my favourite, i shall share them out.
(i'm joking, i'll still do the lot)

and when it hits your oral muscle
that is when the real games start
timing the before, the during
and the after taste's an art.

and sometimes if you cherish it
hang on to one for ages after
while i'm told it's not a drug,
i still get high with post-hit laughter

think of it? i worship it!
i need it very much, it's true
my habit doesn't cost a lot
as i get sent them for review

artisans have started now
to see i truly know their art
i don't eat more than three a day.
and that's unheard of, for a start

i take so long over one box
that i don't need that many, really
but i like to have my shrine,
my stash, and watch it growing, clearly

oh to be a chocolate critic
you can only wonder...
i use my jobs with tender care
and how i love my plunder!

this mourning

i see the shelves
all labouring
under an intense
weight and shame.
i have read
a thousand, more
but never
start to end. i dip.
like we did, intimate...
a stranger now.
my love of the human male
you were the most pure.
i thought
we touched on something
too perfect
it had to be killed
before it died.
or we would,
my poor dead boy,
have felt
worse than
this mourning

wanna hit

feel like getting high tonight
i wanna get real high
i wanna see that violet
i wanna make it fly
i wanna make a bubble blow
away out of my mouth
and puff it into my big dream
then watch it plummet south
i want to forget all this wait
and weigh things up in fire
i want to be attached to colour
gold is cream but higher
i need to be abandoned when
i fall into this mind
if i suppress my ins and outs
i'll weep when i unwind
give me something my amore
give me something harder
let's make some weird potion up
i'll meet you in the larder
where's a candle? hear my mother
"don't have flames they're harmful"
go down to the euro shop
and come back with an armful
let's make powders let's make syrups
let's make magic too
i'm frustrated darling i just
wanna hit with you

freedom of speech

aren't we so lucky?
we've got rather plucky
to be so stable
enough to be able
to say what we
actually really mean...

one is drearily keen
to have one's truth known
to sit on one's throne
and imagine that
anyone act
-ually gives the slightest
fig for one's brightest
illuminations
and what they have been
throughout one's full stream
of thoughts and directions
ones concept-collections
what begins 'when'
then goes on to say 'then'

you drew your conclusions
and dashed their illusions
according to those who will
criticise
then realise
that in your eyes...
they are wrong.

but
not so long
ago
no-one could breach
this freedom of speech
no-one would dare
the spunk wasn't there
they all lived in fear
of what was quite near
or punishment horrid
a come back so torrid

that people said nothing
opinions like stuffing
they kept them all in
they just kept 'em all in

the really odd thing
is that
now we have come round
things have somewhat rewound
we have all this pc
it still isn't easy
so things are remarkably

much as they were.

stop wasting the brown stuff

i truly believe that although we don't eat it
packaging fine *chocolat* has to beat it.
i'd rather taste something my eyes had just cum on
than something blindfolded that just turned my tum on
the lines of the cardboard, the hat box shapes too
the rustle of papers and ballotins seem to
add some sort of magic to what lies inside
it's that which i dream about, ponder with pride.
i think that to have this true love in my heart
is something so lucky, so golden, can't start
to try to go into, attempt to explain
how high i feel there at an artisan's pane
compelled to go in. all the colour, the cases
the detail the artwork the ribbon and laces
this is before i have so much as sniffed,
let alone have inspected each one as a gift.
or purchased or bitten or looked inside, tasted.
undressed chocolate's great. but it's wasted.

i wouldn't live again at sea

i wouldn't live again at sea
what when panic breaks in two
(though it is my home each day)
and land is screaming needy too?

gulls have my name on their beaks
and i can understand them when
they squawk my next task on the earth
is neither related to paint nor pen

nor voice nor body, nor my wit,
my friends, my kin, beloved seed
i'm in waves internally
can't get there now, i would indeed

i hear you birds. i know your will.
i knew it all along and i'll
remain here till i get back home
say it was great, and smile the smile…

content in cream

spread on my couch soft lit in cream
i stumbled on a sort of dream
lying on a feather bed
spirits flew soft spheric head

calm and light unshadowed quite
pulled me on toward the night
i wanted to go somewhere other
floating angst was fit to smother

my white face still pinky hued
and my neck stretched out and cued
to let my hair come falling down
as i arose to find my crown

and kingdom where i'm late to reign
and then i came bright to again.
and realised i live that dream
and *am* soft lit, content in cream.

look

if you look at me once more
i'll make such surfeit of bile
that my mouth will become one big claw.
as you approach me and i smile.
a spray will free flow from before,
disfiguring you forever...
from the sacrum, the plexus, core
your skin dropping off in bits, wherever.
the chair, the air, the floor.

so don't look at me.
not *ever.*

do your worst

so you can bind me
yes right round
again, again
and up and down
like a mummy, ugly string
not embalmed aesthetic binding

you can roll me down the hill
or over rocks or into sea
i cannot know
i cannot see
(and yes, it is a luxury)
it cannot hurt me, cannot go
beyond what i already know
there's nothing worse could ever be for
agony is agony
you get there and you hit the height
there is no worse
you're safe all night

so sew my toes together, go.
it doesn't matter
see the bow
look at this:
the over arch
a dancers foot
there is no starch
they work for years in pain to earn
so they can dance en pointe and turn
with grace and curves
the energy that they all share
we sit, unfit
and watch them there
feeling awkward and in awe
with clammy chocolate on the floor

and you can fill my mouth with earth
but it won't work, i've sung from birth
that beauty was refined and rhymed
for nearly forty years you know?
it does not die

nor suffocate
i won't be absent, even late
i can sing with my mouth full
of anything i care to. oh.
it's all just so
all neat inside
and honed and toned
whale-bodice-boned

you'll have to try much harder, boys
to stop me making so much noise
if you even nearly try
i'll scream up from my womb.
you'll cry.

i smile, as i am rolling free
and singing, dancing
all that's me
and if i never get undone
i'm close to God
and so i've won.

safe

oh heavily, the spasm
bird song stopped and laughter sobbed
munch's screams filled out the chasm

oh heavily it came, the news
and fountains froze and stank of piss
what you wanted, to abuse

oh heavily, she kept her heart

and skies turned yellow grey, burnt
amber
atrophy spread
like forest fires, yes, and red
stalagmites stabbed them all
for what she feared
to give not keep
she'd lost all her beauty
to bitterness.
weep for her.
for her dancing soul smart
for the man that adored her.

oh heavily he was disguarded
suet pudding into swill
oven sooted over perfect meringues
roast lamb grew legs and fur, and ran
it was all wrong
pain will long
for the natural-come-calming conclusion.
a sip of her self-harming infusion

she sliced her nose to ice her face
so heavily she wanted...
safe.

prayers

i pray for other people
the troubled souls i know
i pray for neighbours needing aid
i'm called, so i will go...

i pray for my egyptian friend
whose grandfather is sick
i pray for my bipolar darling
who has been my brick

i pray for all my loved ones
though one of them's a shit
i get down on my knees and sob
and hope they're strong and fit

i pray for both my enemies
i hope that they have changed
nothing meant to harm them so
it's odd. and we're estranged

i pray for all the japanese
caught in their ghastly plight
i want to help them and i will
i make plans in the night

i pray for those who stole my purse
i ask that they're forgiven
(i say that one through gritted teeth
the fact is i am *driven*)

i get my prayers all answered
each one and in its turn
the answer's usually 'no'
you live and then you learn

God's repost is surely right
i trust. i don't "what if?"
for if it weren't part of a plan
i'd dance right off a cliff.

light through it

don't show me your tenderness
when white wings touch my face
please don't put my feelings first
my tears go with your grace

never try to show me
that you mean the words you say
when you revolve around my world
i'm scared i'll lose my way

show me yet your beauty
for i can see the light through it
you make me truly happy
and i'm not used to it

the good news is...

so piss all over my life's work
i couldn't give a monkeys
i've had such worse stuff slung at me
from families of junkies
you only do it to stir things up,
it's witches' caldron hour,
the things you tried to spread and brew
had little or no power
there'll always be some jerk-off type
who wants to leave his mark
the thing is, as with all of life
light triumphs over dark

every time
every time
every time

completely open

the sky looks down on lovely purple
reds and mauves around me now
you can't take live colours from me
they're to be as leaves to bough

they all emanate from spirit
one majestic forest towers
so much time to fill with poems
songs and paintings, edible flowers

you can't take my ring off either
not because it's too caressing
it belongs there, it is emma
not accessory, nor dressing

when i smile you feel it, don't you?
yes, you know that i can sense
every tiny speck of dust fall
from the big blue, no defence!

zero fun

i won't forget
you never do
my sheer dismay
and chagrin too...

when mummy said
that for a treat
we could buy
a special sweet

all the shops
were featuring
new fun sized bars
and i was *teetering*
on the edge all day.

then, they were there.

and i was just
in sheer despair

so little me
went into one.
they'd made that something
zero fun

they were just...
much *much* smaller?

violets

violets will now give praise to the wild asparagus

it came inside,
in a green shiny new bucket
while it was glistening
"just with its own joy
of being a thing"
i think, as i drink
my third cup of tea

but they stayed out there

i wanted to pick them
but i held back
i thought i could feel
where they wanted to be
free, and
almost invisible
droplets of inside-crown royal velvet
in a pool of millais green

i want to be violet
almost unseen
so they can just sense me
i suggest vent vert, wine,
a song and a rose
and tears enough
to grow next year's
grass

the sun is a given
the smile never is...

for mothers

look at your hands
put inside them
all of Christmas' goodness

decorations, spices
carols, myrrh
mulled wine, charity

squeeze them together
sob for an hour or so
and look inside your hands

are they empty?
or are they full?
and if so, of what?

you made that.

the second step

starting to move on again.
like light rain
upon spring's first crocus,
soft sweet exhalation,
damp relief on His floral cloudy cobalt.

the sudden moody skies above,
now what will they deliver?
if that is a flash of corn-gold sun
that might be coming hither...?

if so i will run, bare foot and rapid
and gather up all the village kids
and we will do a rainbow dance.
all of us together:

singing, jumping and playing, yes!
our little feet drumming, the candour of grass,
whisperings of deep belief
that God is here. i'm sure, at last

why don't italians
(all die from smoking non-stop from about birth?)

smoking is a sly old beast
creeps up on one so craftily
and now it's banned in inner space
and so they drag on draftily

but why make something good so bad
and why make suffering pot luck
i dabbled with it years ago
and now it's beckoning, the suck

and inhalation, helping one
to loosen up one's coiled spring
i'll not be slaved, but there is
such perfection in the packaging

they offer me, i say "i don't"
all squared and cellophane and foil
what about live for today?
so please God, help with my recoil.

in italy i do believe
it's in the law, you *have* to smoke
from little girl in skinny jeans
to city worker and her bloke

this town wins, i want it all
these monied folk with hermes bags
are ruled by it! there's ergonomic
inbuilt pockets for their fags...

it ticks me off. it's true. and you
would see yourselves, and you'd concede.
my theory is they're all laid back
it's *stress* that kills you, not the weed.

the power of picking out the softies

i see you, other person
all curled up seated there
when i go in or out of church
and wonder if we're there.

to use your picture of Maria
as a bargain tool...
to flick heart strings of blood all over
those big steps, with your next fool.

to flood shit pity, have your day
go home with 90 euro
i go inside and try to pray.
at home inside my bureau

is 18 for our weekly shop.
well done, today you did your worst.
you know your every cue and cry
just hearing you my day was cursed.

your gift is sharp, you use it well
my gift's my art, my love, my fears.
yours is sniffing out the ones
who'll spend their rest of day in tears.

rising above it

oh jealousy, oh sorest envy
don't come here for me to feed you
it's just need, you didn't choose me
i need you to need me, too

comfort

i know a man who hurts so much
he's distracted, goes deep
he gets so low
but i see in him the truth, so much
that i always comfort him so:

i just say this
"hush, my darling, there's nothing to stir you up tonight
rest your troubled head
and let's ride that stallion sleep together"

i tell him fighting himself must be wrong
he says i feel what is mostly heard
"can you relax for me, be strong?"
he says i soothe him with my words
he says that i soothe him with my words,
and with my mouth

i just say this:
"hush, my darling, there's nothing to stir you up tonight
rest your troubled head
and lets ride that stallion sleep together"

he says he has no home to go
that his vision is lost, from fear.
he says *he's* lost
so i say "i know
but there is always room for you here, you know?
i tell you,
there's always room for you at my hearth
in my home"

...and then he holds me
so desperately
and in that powerful dance,
the transformational blue source of the firelight
he's a woman
he has become a woman for me
reaching out as far as a woman will reach for comfort...

the wrong book

the kids in line all books in hand
the book store it was heaving
though no-one seemed to filter in
and dozens they were leaving...
the authoress was writing names
and one of them was hers
bag on table, books in bag
she talked with kids in verse!

it was far too crowded for us
(truth it shall be told here)
and after hours it was our turn
at last we were near...
we got our squiggles, and both names
and went home high and pleased
she even took a pic of her
they both were so at ease!

pass me mummy's pink pills please...
in-store it went sick-fizzy
with zillions of five year olds
her desk-books-bags-phone busy.

at home, and comforting ones child
"we'll find another book-store..."
 for dedicated to my babe:
"the big hole duty of a whore"

purple sweet wrapper in my pocket

i saw that sea
or rather heard it
smelled like
one big rush of life.

what had been numb
what had been dead
now had become
chainsaw lead
hacking through my every nerve
and up between my legs
and out
through the top of my head

more n more boxed drugs they push
to try to shut me up.
chemical warfare
inside my brain

if they can't cure you
they'll make you look mad
then false, having failed
so they don't look bad

what i had:
two loving parents
a pair of wellies, a woolly hat...
and a purple sweet wrapper
in my pocket, just that
at that time
just that.
the purple ones are just the tops
they are mahatma ghandi
(chain-eat 8 at all times of stress
trust me cos on this, i do know best)

words and all of their power escaped me
mute with it all
in black not navy
the real deal
fear fear fear

like ink blot vomiting blood in his office
see what you see in the twenty-eighth smear

or maybe
i had just needed
to express and be heard ...

the vast wild undressed me, understood
i liked to conduct with my baton of driftwood
the symphonic sympathy, the sacred water
i knew i was my maestro neptune's fair daughter

and often could stop me
from spiralling down
like feisty fossils
attention seekers on the shore
the diehard ladies, bald that boast
"i'm 83, you know"
but these, they can add millions to that
the starlets of the sea shore show!
with nets and ginger beer cans
from years back
that eczema with time
what survivors *we all are* here today!
one kicks them around
as i kick myself but
not this time, no
not this time

i'm going down again...
not again Lord, no
it'd been ok for 20 minutes here
"dad, help! one's coming over..."
"then listen to the sea my darling
listen hard"
i did and i smiled
i ran ran ran 'til i could run no more...
collapsed and giggled, lifted up from the core

drugs see-sawing in my brain that needed calm
not turbulence, artifice,
one size fits all
and some don't make it...

dungeness, *you saved my life*
when i could not communicate
it's real, the sea, it spoke to me!
and it sounded like low distant mermen
urging me "no, live on, emma
wait for your worthy destined will-be
grow into who you *will* be
you will write too
ay, me…you shiny spirit!"

i bent over on my daddy
a tall lean body, a total support
my baby, my lover, my husband these years
hanky all sicky
shirt sodden in tears
who told me the time
three minutes past smoked fishy three
"he'll ring me now"
that line was mine.
time.

stop.

and jarman's house
had me safe and assured
that if i lived on i wasn't so alone
and if i just couldn't
i'd meet some folk up there
i said he would ring (the bullshitter slater),
he left his limp message…
three minutes past three
that i found out later
oh waste of time, message
oh waste of time, he
but i'd meet some great folk…
oh yes, that would be!

i stayed alive
but jarman died
and dad and i go back there
sometimes inside

my salumiere's gone

i heard just yesterday the news
that our salumiere's gone.
he'd always painstakingly choose
the best for me, his soul just shone

he must have been, oh, sixty five?
and worked hard every day i bet
but he made me feel more alive
than most people i've ever met

he didn't know my name, nor i
knew his, it wasn't how we were
he cut the meat and i would buy
he chortled when i called him 'sir'

it's just like life, you find the thing
that makes your day, you like it so
sometimes he would make me sing
for one more etto of prosciutto!

then you lose it. and it's blank.
that space is filled with something duller
that old chap was the top rank
and gave my paint board one new colour

he had a way with him that spoke
of *you*, not *me*, he seemed to care
he was a life-affirming bloke
and from now on, he won't be there…

what if the best thing were to happen

post prandial perfection.
though it was… what?
letting the little light in
allowing all the "we don't want any of that,
thank you" to squeeze out of
the gap in the old pine door
the one i wanted you said no
and you were right
at the time yes, so
coax it out just as it is
bilious belly bulge out of weeny wood skirt
then turn round, and come back to us
fine and pure
statuesque streaming sensuality
see how your
childhood expectations
held up:

"you were right"

it can't be true!
so God is good...
and i needn't have worried
heavily and endlessly
and wept all night
and hid behind make up
and over exuberance
and over given
and tried so hard

i could have just
borne my name
and

been me

flat white light

what is this thing, i've no conception
of it now. or my perception's
gone and done a runner here
in search of flat white light, i fear.
make some clues creep forth to me
there's not a lot that i don't see
i don't miss much i'm awfully bold
but this one makes me thin, out-rolled
like pastry as you punish it
turn it into sheets to fit
in any pan or tin you'll use
and now i'm getting low, confused
i've heard of radiant bright light
and moody shades and sunny bright
but flat and white make me feel sick
can't see it. *someone* has the trick
or they would not have called it so.
can't cope with this. i gotta go.

half a clock face, half a life (for emilia romagna)

04.04 same as my birthday
our bed is moving around in my dream
ice skates on a skating rink
buried under my reality screen
and the floor does not support
but the ground it *should* support!
he grabs my hand
"earthquake, my darling"
wearing black silk nightie, socks
we enter the grand atrium
chandeliers swing back and forth
like the ones in the park for the kids.
and we are both sick
toilet, sink.

the tv goes on
it's all over the news
richter 6
like l'aquila
all those missing souls remembered
7 missing so far here…
it will be ever more they say
far more that that

disorientating

and it's totally quiet outside
ghost town,
normally so full of cheer
people laughing
glasses crashing
phone calls through the night.
not here.

then another
then one more
more ice skating furniture
and another
more they come
less horrific
still, you don't want it
and more sick

i'm very sick
but i make tea
because i'm english
that is how we won the war.
hysteria he had no place here
no tears
no tangles
not a trace

our families all call for us
we call them all
i send them emails
so they don't die
when they hear
the reportage
i save them that heart-stopping moment
when you know.
you just know.
i tell them i'm alive, ok.
apart from my stomach
and shaking limbs
he's the same
we cannot sleep
the earth moved without our love-making
there is no humour in this at all.

i look for none
i would not court it
if it should come
to me on a chance

my beloved red arched city
bolognese dreams are here
then we see the pictures coming
a violated,
raped old building
they died there
they lost their might
a ruinous castle
now just rubble
it's not real
but it is life.

trouble for my eyes, my senses brewing
hyper stimulation cooing

i am stoic in a crisis
but this is new for me,
you see...
i come from an island where
we are not used to terror
really

and there it is.
the front page image
half a belltower
half a clock
like the half lives
stolen from their families.
people living half their clock
my face, it is half a face, too
my guilt at living
my joy at being saved
my poor stomach
in waves of pain
my bologna will never be the same
it's split from twelve to seven
so
not even half a clock will show

we don't sleep
i have a nightmare
it was in my system though.

i felt this coming
for several days
i felt an omen
rising in me
striking up a dreadful image
not for me
but blatantly
so bad for everyone, the sea
the earth, the sun, and planetary
yes and even history.

restless emma
feeling nothing
knowing why
but knowing nothing
i knew nothing
something gruesome

ugly, hurting
manic me

bologna is regal and red and elegant
bologna was regal and red and elegant

death toll rising
it can't be
say it's not
that it's just me...
me and my hypersensitivity

not even half a bell tower standing
half is proud and half is crumbled
like the face of the one you love
when you tell them
you are dying,
and it will be in pain...

half a clock face
half a bell tower
half an hour of sleep for me
half a clock
not even half
and half lives for those
whom we will remember

and the bats in the bell tower
knew all along
i heard it all
i knew their song
but if i'd dared a friendly warning
they'd have thought that i was mad(-der)
and not have changed their actions so
what chance had we ever had?
for only animals know before
something seismic comes to pass
but the bats knew, so did i
wipe grit deeper into my eye

half a clock face
half mine too
bologna
this i write for you

weeping willow

i saw a weeping willow and
approached with high heels on
i didn't care if they would wash
i needed to belong

noise

the fridge does battle with the kitchen clock
just to be heard, in single voice
instead we have a nightmare mix of
tasteless noises in an empty space.

so they have gone now. all gone now.
i am alone with my boots off, my eyes
heavier with each passing drip,
a trio of
domestic empty words...
please shut up you solo pip
i know what you think of me
you've all gone now
but you never shut up
you just never shut up
personal sounds ringing in my senses
i know what you do and
i'm bored by it.

she says "we all have our battles in life"
"some more than others", i think and with force
he's at the dentist, i hope they don't hurt him
i hear that vile screeching, and in pain the fourth

flea ridden dog's gone bananas below,
and baby makes six. my breasts hurt now.
i wanted the church bells but what i got is
tasteless noises in an empty space

if i were a man

if i were a man
who wanted me
i'd seek out
what i find lovely

send white roses,
blood ones too
buy a chagall,
one in blue

i would fill
a box with truffles
darkest chocolate
tied with ruffles.

i'd fantasize
look out for clothes
adorn my muse
from neck to toes

i'd write love letters
and in verse
i'd lie, all show
i'd put *me* first

and play tricks
to get my way
and then resort to
fouler play

i'd start with insults
spread some lies
i'd tell them all she'd
spread her thighs

if i were a man
that's how i'd be
that's how they are
when they want me

this sunday's gathering

caramel touches a splurge of gold
and creamily drifts me away into peace
upside down and slightly sick if i resist
gorgeous in gauze when i give myself up
lying a-hammock of lilac and honeysuck
scent pulls you further and further along
and deep into drowsiness that is your centre
when nothing feels awkward and love is your plexus.
if i were to paint it i'd melt every colour
each sun would melt into each moon...
her head would be high and supported held back
as she were receiving the waviest liquid
melted from inside the silver spoon.
i chose this sunday because it felt written
i felt this day wouldn't be long forgotten
and one of us went right to heaven and back.
one stayed there for good. so i guess i was right.

tea and cake

the heaviness pushes its nothingness upon me... its lightness too can be a pressure... it's 109 degrees here today, the sun always shines on tv though... oh no, i'm at home just practising my act, that's right... "camera-men? you there? no. yoo-hoo? no? no. good"... silence... i can have a chocolate, make tea and dangle my legs out of the window, it makes for a nice "staying the same"... a same is as good as a rest....to rest, to rest at last, the utter joy of knowing the odd thoughts have started, that sure sign that sleep is coming and will steal your reasoning... and you are alone with your reason for waking up and getting up or not...

the joy, the joy, *the joy* that i felt when i first saw our flat, and knew it was perfect, or would be soon, the joy of a cup of tea straight from the leaves in my much loved easter bunny pot, in old english china mugs, or a thin porcelain cup and matching saucer with dainty violets or lilies. that first sip, my trip to paradise.

i told you i'd go through with it if you weren't nice, you didn't quite believe me, because i'm so sensitive. i couldn't harm a fly could i? but i did, i did, *i did*... i am like a peach you see: a rosy skin, all smooth and soft, and sweet, sweet juice, like nectar from the gods, flesh so delicious that it's indecent to eat in public and tender too inside your mouth when you chew... and inside there is a stone, hard as a rock and equally as old... you can be both you know, sensitive and tough... and so i bring to you weight and lightness, my two friends, and watch one day they'll make amends, they can work well when playing together, when compliant, dough and feather... oh no. it's happening again, the talking in poetry thing, i try not to do it, i try not to forget english words too, but it happens, it's happening more n more, and one looks utterly pretentious, and it's all frightfully boring...

my tea is cold... makes me feel violent... having the first sip and not burning my tongue, that is cold to me, you see? *and that is how life is for me.* there's little worse though, he needs money, what can i do but look at his honey and give him anything he needs? these drugs are good, they are indeed... and they cost in so many ways, but by migraine day 9, i've gone astray... no pain is here... i have put my mind to something else...

so i'm baking a cake for my friends graduation. it's taking hours, and it shall have 5 tiers, a square, an oval, a triangle, a round and a little star for the top... graded, as she was, as they go up they get smaller... and they will all be different colours too, pastel shades i think for her, but they will all taste of real roses... i'll get them from my brother in spain, he'll send them over, he'll be there for me, then for the top, a dark chocolate sauce to be heated just until it's warm... i'll pour it over my bit first just to check its not poisoned... it will be for elisa or *für elise* you might say (if you were socially awkward/ insecure or trying to impress)... the heaviness pushes its nothingness upon me... its lightness too can be a pressure...

i don't know for certain why i killed him, i think it was based around irritation mounting up for months, i said, "if you call me hours late, having made a date, making me wait, one more time..." and he did. so i went to his house, a few hours away, and i took it out of my suspender belt and sat on his lap, legs astride him, in his georgian arm chair, and said "i've got a surprise for you", i'd taken a tablet to take just the edge off such an 'unusual' evening, and i'd put it inside my mouth and sucked it off slow up and down and i'd winked at him - now, c*learly* i'd dipped it in melted 89% cocoa solids dark chocolate first - and he said "don't do it, i know that you want me, think of the sex that i'd miss with you gone", he took the gun from my mouth, put it in his, and looked at at me, sucked it (*revolting*, repulsing me), up and down, up and down, he held it by the shaft making it *really* easy for me, i said "unbelievable, you're *such a man*" (groaning, grinding up and down) "i told you not to keep me hanging on, life is short, plus it's plain bad manners," and then i got excited and angry and raised my singer's voice to a scream "is your time more important than mine? who am i, nothing? no darling, i'm gold dust and now... you're just dust" i shot the gun into his mouth three times. *three* feeling betters. *three* redressing the balance, *three* becoming a murderess, which turned me on... (you learn a thing a day) i enjoyed myself all over his corpse and thought of how thin the sex/ violence line can be. women have to have a reason for sex. men just need a place. the power of a woman. the powerlessness of a man. the love i have for my family. so. they must never know. it wouldn't go down well at their local church... the heaviness pushes its nothingness upon me... its lightness too can be a pressure...

i hope elisa likes her cake.

for hastings and its incredible gift

we are used to fighting, winning
can you hear what i can hear
tumbling over and over each other
waves split-crashing on our pier?

it was like a girl on fire
whipping whirling dervish dancers
orange blood red clouds at night-time
thank God neptune's cease-fire answered.

the cards they dealt us, hot with horror.
great britannia rules the waves
cradle the wreckage we once sang on
we're in charge, we won't be slaves.

the gentle sounds of power rising
from the farthest reach of sands
driftwood, ice cream, fish huts, cobbles
tell us we don't know his plans.

we have this gift of re-creation.
art was hastings, way back then.
and when we make this joy together
we see our pier rise again!

sorry lot

we are well fed, have far too much
we've got it all and still we moan
a sky scraper just fits the screen
of model 53 iphone

they were oppressed enslaved abused
but when they sing in church it's *joy!*
they dwell on what they have, so they can
give God's kid a shiny toy

he killed six million of their faith
the sun shines sweet on husks of corn
and yet their *jokes* are just the best.
that's humour in it richest form.

we're too well fed, we're fat and ill
we've been so spoilt from the cot
and *our* hymn singing's flat and dull
in general we're a *sorry lot*

in neptune's arms

i'm walking fast along the tide
running very nearly
i feel the wet chill through my top
it's pornographic really.
i listen to vaughan williams and his
theme on thomas tallis
i wish to tell the world today
i drink from that same chalice.
my mind is square with painful corners
monday it was bubbled
everything was soft and see-through
now its sorely troubled.
i saw a man do something bad
and felt such utter shame
for in one set of circumstances
i'd have done the same...
i'm slowing down, it's at my waist
this water will be home now
i lost my music way back but
it's pushing me on somehow...
they say the salty taste and smell
it's viscous, stabs your nose
but i feel it's the natural way
it's how the blue grass grows.
i'm floating face down out to sea
it's perfect footage really
so film me, safe in neptune's arms
i did my best. sincerely.

mine

there's not enough canvas in the world
to hold my dreams, still for all time
or paper leaves or serviettes
to store those endless thoughts of mine

stalla

i need to be in the stalla tonight
low down and touching the floor
lie on a rug or a blanket. no
i don't want anything more

i want the minimum gift in time
i need to feel my solid earth
i can't be floating around any more
it made me sick, that salty surf

i want to be drinking water here
not champagne, nor vodka, nor wine
i want a real fire if i am cold,
to be naked whenever i'm fine

i don't wanna be just a wanna-be
i want no more than i deserve
i just want my lover here next to me
to be loved and oh yes, to serve.

pre

roses are red
violets are… ooh.
i'm not pre orgasmic
i just need the loo

before i go

silent kitchen
too much air
everybody's
had their share
set for thirteen.
no-one there

i am sitting looking on
they don't know where i belong
from the outside looking in
who am i, where i have been?

i'm not sure
that i know either
guess one's soul knows both
and neither

i think i'd like
someone to know.
it might be nice,
before i go

her poem

look at her wings, and how fragile they are...
you can see through them, bend down and look up
moving your arms in that way is an angel
who sewed up her lips, but now drinks from the cup.
look at her flowing hair back in waves falling
billowing surging soft surf on the pink
it stays as in clear water smoothly confusing
your feeling, that slow struggle with what you think.
look at her body, what does it excite in you
envy in reverence, magic in cloud?
you try to touch it but back away crying
instinctively knowing you won't, though allowed
look at her eyes, it's my mother, my father
it's God in his half form, true beauty, sad sighing.
she doesn't blink, all her motion is dancing
and singing and writing and loving and lying

you came at two cos one was not right… you have juice stains on your blanket and smell of sweet straw…

oh God, it's coming the great wave of time… who are you? …divine little thing… there are snakes everywhere in the grass here you know, be careful, oh Lord, can i mother you? can i get fat with you, then push you out into the world, then cradle you, feed you my milk, give you my whole heart, my every minute, and love love love you… you could grow up with me, play with me, sing with me, dance with me… i long to nurture you… i long to be your mummy… watch your unique character emerge… let me give you treats and spoil you with all the right things…

oh God, it's coming, the great wave of time… let me hold you. you look as helpless as i used to feel… but no, you are safe here and so am i, the clouds are calling us, baby, they tell us to hope for more, and expect less, they tell us rhymes that don't have endings, they tell us being high is healthy when it's natural

oh, God it's coming, the great wave of time, they tell us to go amid the hay and straw and look for the needle as if to find, don't prick yourself, little one, tell mummy and she will pick it up for you, we must picture finding it with all of our might, i bet if my mother wanted to find it, even in a bail as big as her palace, *she* would, she *would*, she would, you know. let's work within this game, oh darling, it's all right, you're with me, in my arms… can you hear the clouds talking, darling, bursting with truth, information about the sun and the moon? …your new world! even if utopia were offered to me now, i would rather stay with you, my baby… and then we have grandad to consider, our fine, genius, handsome pop. how you will sit on his knee and bounce and he will make you giggle and tickle you, and you can make him watch disney and i will howl with laughter as wagner is his thing, really… he will worship you from the word "*gooo*"… you will love his close connection with you, he is mine too… the clouds keep on chatting, how do you hear them, low and booming, or normal, just smudged up? they tell you you're safe now, that i am your mummy, they tell you genetics can be manufactured

oh God, it's coming the great wave of time… they tell you that "do re mi" is always curative, clouds come and cuddle you if you get cold, just like your cream coloured blanky, yes, just like a duvet, my arms will never be anywhere else but round you, my little thing, my sweet little fudge piece. my breasts are suddenly terribly swollen and my nipples are toughening inside my cotton dress, my ugly beauty never more radiant all cos of you... money is nothing, we have none i tell you, but mummy will give you everything you need... you will want for nothing... and mummy knows secrets you'll so love to learn...

oh God, it's coming, the great wave of time... clouds tell me stories and then tell me more facts "did you know jfk was in agony most of his life?" "how is this relevant to my new baby?" "it isn't, i just thought it was interesting" ...clouds tell me *you are mine*. we're family. cloudy the truth, no, it shines through like laser... baby, so perfect, baby, the fledgling the little robin nesting, nests in my bosom and feed from me there... you look up to me when you take me in your mouth, with your biggest brown eyes, and i love you more than my life, you see... you look after me just with your faith in me...

oh God, it's coming the great wave of time... don't walk in bare feet... oh! you can't walk at all yet! how old are you, two or three weeks at the most? mummy was worrying unnecessarily... snakes in the grass., watch out when you're older, they're everywhere, they come with life i'm afraid... but the roses, the daffodils, they are all over the earth you will see, and for now you'll like engines, and train tracks and thomas, i guess... your voice is so wonderful, you sound like you're bleating, and when you want feeding i'll know, i can feel it. mama was a bad girl but now is a good girl and i never hurt *anyone* intentionally... we have our morals, we have our codes and we have our family, it starts you and me... i wonder if anyone makes up fairy tales makes up high jinxes and fantasies now... the clouds are like pillows, they find you, they find you, they told me to look under the sweet william at two, so i did... and here you are, my love, an angel gurgle little boy... we need to wash you i think... and we do... i'll wash you under the fresh spring of water where they go once a week for their demi-john refills and then we take you to the sacred water up in the hills in lucca, in tuscany... there we arrive, and there i unbutton you... and as i wash you in the holy water, i see that you're a baby girl! ...the clouds didn't tell me that, not a word. this is so like life. i am getting that 'yes' feeling this is so right

oh God! it's coming the great wave of time... fill me up here... always the days when you don't expect anything are the ones when you get your ice cream or big film... i got my clouds and my baby girl too... i am overflowing with joy. i have never felt this level of happiness. i am going to die. i said that when he last made love to me. no i will stay alive in it, sustain it without effort... oh God, a new me! i shan't swear any more. they left you here for me to raise you and will i? *will i?* i will never let go of you, never lose sight of you, you will have everything i couldn't have! ... you won't be taken away from your daddy, nor beaten in fear by your mother's lover, nor anything bad , you'll never hear ugly things above you at night, holding the pillow over your ears, or see your mother sobbing for years on the stairs. you will be perfectly bathed in scented jasmine and uncle jaime from catalonia will feed you fresh edible flowers from his fields, and uncle antonio from london will take you to carluccio's for chocolate cake, and daddy and i here in bologna will paint with you and have fun all day long... thank you, God, for sending the clouds today, for giving me pain, for taking all my hope away... now it's five billion times sweeter, the joy of my baby girl, i'll call you talitha, for you are my little star

oh God! it's coming the great wave of time... oh, oh! the clouds tell me now that we both need a rest and i'm all wrapped around you, ready for your needs when you wake up hungry or tearful or giggling... i never cried at your age, you know, i started at 16 and then didn't stop for 24 years... but now i shall laugh for the rest of my life. *i know that i will*, for God tells me so... and the clouds are now telling me they have to go... they have to go... they have to go...

after effects

need a cotton wool fluff ball
or something soothing on my brow
a gentle, soft thing, giving out
ok-ness with what happens now

need a calmness never felt
at deeper levels through me
a dandelion meditates
affirming that it is to be

need a hand to stroke-hold mine
oh! how i long to touch and reach
as many as i can, give hope...
and stroke the down of peach, *yes*
to stroke the down of a peach

fella from fife

i fancied this fella from fife
and fantasized 'bout being his wife
i drugged him up daily
he wed me quite me gayly
he's gay. but you just get one life.

i called my snowman 'cloud'

when i was young
i don't know how
but four or five
i feel somehow?
there was thick snow.
of course my plan
was set to make
a fine snowman.
i nipped upstairs
my 'secret' sweet -
the last one - would
be *cloud*'s to eat
he loved it, too
my 3 coal button,
sticks and carrot nose,
for mum's mutton...
pop's pipe, flat cap
cloud was taking on
a character of his own...

it took hours
he was so fat
and i was smiling
"i did that!"

the next day was
the very worst one
my tears were ice
in the bright sun

i thought that if i
fed him magic
he would stand
forever.

tragic.

salt dust

to feel the prick of
salt dust in my eye
is to know for sure
i am home again

rainbow towers

(a game given to me at my kindergarten by father christmas in 1973. a little boy had wanted it, as well as his gift, so he scratched me, and i still have a scar on my right thigh. it grew with me. we still have that 'rainbow towers' and its a great game. it grew with me too).

i don't sit and think before i write.
i open my computer top
and turn it on and just tune out
the images flood in, don't stop

i work the other way, i think
i lazily loll out of window
half an hour with blank inside
my mind is off. but red, full flow.

more like trying *not* to write
that's hard for me. and *not* to paint.
that same control *not* to begin the
feast before you, feeling faint.

i can't stop the ideas coming.
how long must this have been brewing?
i just know it's being open
what a dove sparks off by cooing

i mostly don't have trouble sleeping
i can sit stone still for hours
but when i let my channels open
i am off. my rainbow towers!

nobody knows

she comes from the wilds of her own imagination
but where she is going nobody knows

watch her eating fruits from the gods
they lift under her chin
her hair flies back
they place one piece in her dark mouth
lying as they will on their left hip sides
she smiles, tongue crashing into one more berry
coated in spirit and sensuality
look at them longing for a sigh or a gesture
they pop another jewel in
and long for her to speak

she comes from the wilds of her own imagination
but where she is going nobody knows

watch her drinking nectar clear
from a cup of botticelli blue
everything's in gold and red
how they wipe under her lip when the swallow's flown...
she will only look down mildly
they are lolling on the clouds
feel their hot desire for her
virgin, blonde and un-sucked breasts
she is draped in pale green muslim
she's organic in their feast
hear the gods sigh as they give her
gifts of something
that's not love, but linked

she comes from the wilds of her own imagination
but where she is going nobody knows

then she slowly raises half an eye
straight ahead
they all stoop down
just to see what colour they are
they think violet, i know they're olive
and i know from what will she refrain...
she slowly raises up one arm,

they are simply caught.
set in her net and in her gaze now
fifty of them squirm in awe
at her beauty
in its pure fragility
dark green eyes turn left hip right hip
turning over their big boulders in the white

"he who knows what i'm desiring
give that to me and i am yours"

she comes from the wilds of her own imagination
but where she is going nobody knows

painter

there once was an artist, a painter
who let life nor touch her nor taint her
but she bought some varnish
and turps for the tarnish
and now she's a bit of a fainter

in search of good news

i was searching through the journal
for good news, a task eternal
it was all diana's dresses
how her life was full of stresses
i was sick and slow with it
i was bored, the room ill-lit
it was suicidal weather
rain and mist on english heather
earl grey was my solace then
so i indulged myself again
i needed some such sustenance
to help me stay up on the fence
before i fell with pure frustration
train stuck endlessly in station.

then i saw something so foul
so gross and ugly, made me howl
inside and right onto the broadsheet
i stumbled off my two numb feet
i had sat so long in waiting
unwittingly participating
in a tiny three line square
as if it were not even there
"earthquake in india" it read
"two hundred thousand people dead"

thief

you place into your cabinet
my gorgeous golden egg
look at me here on my uppers
far too proud to beg.
you stole it from me, short, ugly boy.
the sea sweeps in some scum
a mermaid sits and weeps for me
she knows what is to come.
you have so many other pieces
why did you want mine?
i worked for it, i ooze three lakes
of salty ocean brine:

the one is for the mermen
a gift of joy they win,
the second is for dad to drink,
the third to drown you in.

i do not mean to, but i do

i check for messages every hour
i do not mean to, but i do
it's just like gazing at a flower
wanting blossom to push through

you said that if don't hear
from you every day or night
all it means is you're caught up,
or busy. something light.

not that you've gone off it all
and changed your subject, broken word
or that you have had the call
to kill a muted mocking bird

i fear to phone or drop a line
i'm scared that it might irritate
but then if i don't show you mine
might *your* care then depreciate?

i check for messages every hour
i do not mean to but i do
i'm drowning in slow motion now...
stuck with one sick image of you.

creation

the rain comes down, with urgency
and strikes the roses 'til a petal sheds
we always use liquid and sticky abuse
to make more of our myriad flower beds

what hair-dos do

when a woman has her hair done
she becomes a different girl
hard to explain to those who don't
but joy is in each cut or curl
she looks just like she wants to feel:
free, and in control and rich.
she might put shades on just to tease
behind them she might be a bitch.
she may just catch a man today,
or spend it at home cooking.
either way she'll be empowered
just cos she *feels* good looking.

set her free

in my cupped hands a rose today
just petals, but no core
i wondered if it felt like me
some pieces, nothing more.

last of the snow

i went to church
but it was closed
(on a sunday)
so i stood and posed

for photographs
my emerging
from reclusion
with some urging

from the others
walking ahead
i hang back
it has been said

and what was before me
all soot and muddy
the last of the snow
just like that bloody

fella who cheated me
stole my last pink
and left me with nothing
but time to think

i lifted my foot high
to kick his head in
but new leather boots...

so i thought of him
dead
instead.

miss diamond

oh you, miss diamond
pure as snow
nothing can touch you
no-one can harm
you and your infinite virginity.

no imperfect wretched human
could sully your *quite brilliant* white.
shine like a tear of love afterwards...
a trickle of joy during...
or glassy eyes a moment before...
liquid miss diamond, yes this jewel
this perfect reflection of sex
withstands the knocks and scrapes of time
you mirror the moment the moon was made
with joy with joy with joy!

like love, she lives on through disaster
he told me that
and so it is.

pour onto me your glass-mined gloss
paint some class on horror, what?
miss diamond withstands pain and fire
mental torture, glass splintered mind...
smashing, razor, cutting beauty glass.

it's never something out of reach
you may see perfection now
it's here, right on my finger.
God made it.

i thank you, both.

push it

she can't know this
only *she* can
she thinks that it's hard
it's not

this one knows
they feel it deeper
this one knows she'll
feel like rock

he can't push it
only *he* can
push it 'til his bones
split through

we can't give it
only *we* can
we *could*
but we never do

perverted

i've worked it out at forty two
i've done the maths here, as you do
i can very clearly see
what was worse than greek to me
that this is how it goes, it seems
in daytime waking and in dreams
that when the world is full of fear
i'm the one who's steadfast here
and when they're having fun and idle
i'm most often suicidal

all those that can't swim stand on chairs

i place six chairs around a room
tears in black mascara offer themselves up to you,
male, human,
like a pretty, well spoken virgin with pert nipples
fluttering her eye lashes
saying "take me"
i wasn't even wearing any...
this charcoal must be coming up
from decades ago.
a girl who is a weakish swimmer
needs protection
but still needs freedom
i must have freedom

so i change chair...

i stretch out, like a ballerina
from the one onto the next.
me
and six chairs.
all girl guests.
women stretching, breasts, buttocks, naked,
strung out, hanging on
begging for help
6 guests, all me,
and an ocean in the kitchen...

streaks of long wet hair everywhere

lily

roaming rolling petals, lovers
assorted designers
all different colours

i dare myself, draw you into my space
the weirdest one
the one in disgrace

come, queeen of flowers, bend to me
i let your strangeness live inside...
it won't hurt, trust me, you will see

so let it in, inside was tight
i opened up
as i do when i write

so penetrate me, fill me in
feminine floristry swallowing juice
perfume, silk shell, gossamer, wing

i'm joyfully sensing your lack of shame
and do you know, lily
i feel the same.

deliver us

i saw a speck and went for it
and caught it with my clench
i opened up and what i found
was thirst i couldn't quench

nothing was there, air and nothing
just an empty palm
longing for a spirit, sun-flake
dandelion arm

i needed there to be some stardust
or a fragile wing
purple elfin or a secret
message coded in something

i wanted more. i needed more
i do, please God don't leave me
lying here, alone with my imagination?
...perilous. but feed me!

carried off in breeze

i saw a window to my left
or was it jagged sunlight
hurt my hair to be so dizzy
something shone so bright

i thought i'd wash my hair just then
it often cools a headache over
when i stood below the water
i was rolling down in clover

field was massive, daisy strewn
but i was not alone
people dressed in orange cried
and made a massive moan

i know i'm good at comforting
i went to offer aid
they didn't see me there at all
and i became afraid

i walked through them and into sands
the sort before a sea
i saw a clear reflection
in the water. wasn't me.

it was a pelargonium
quite bold and standing tall
i loved my blossom but my stalk
was blue and like a ball

i felt my seeds and wondered
if i had a rare disease
it did upset me but the angst
was carried off in breeze

...carried off in breeze

flying

throw my hair back far, and drink from the chalice
i love my enemies; goodwill, no malice
smiling at strangers but that's nothing strange
i like to give of myself at close range.

i don't feel bony or puffy or wrong
i just feel so glad to be singing my song
and i want to burst cos i hear his sweet sound
so many orgasms within one mound

i am a woman as such i am strong
right in the present though nothing is wrong
all of the movement and costume and paint
i want to cry out with joy but i'm faint

that is quite normal i'm often found crying
but i'm mother earth *and* her muse when i'm flying.

the fourth poem

today i cannot interact
i cannot quite be bothered
i want to lie here bathed in love
and write, just write,
again and again
receiving free fall from above

always the ideas come
i am owned by love
and by the muse
i know that God feels fine with this
because
he had her choose

i want to paint
to make amends with hell
i created on friday.
can't find it in me
to move from here
this day it shall be my day

i want to sing
but that's downstairs
and in my studio
i love it down there
it's my haven
but today can't do so

and so i lie abed and talk
to foreign readers
i don't know
i love the fact
that within months
they will catch my throw

today i cannot interact
d'you ever get
this way?
but i will need to busy up
and keep my demons
sound at bay

rampant scarlet

red and crimson, damson orange
violent hot coals, blazing garnet
walking slowly over fire
don't look at your feet, you twit

it's all said now
walk the walk
your
want want want's
not good enough, sir dim

effort, hours, sweat and trial
heat wave of determined searing
wanting is pathetic, listen!
weedy, wilting, simpering, fearing

rampant scarlet fights the fight
that girl always gets it right.

oil seed rape

i walked across the field today
the calm and joy within me was overwhelming
i smiled
alone
only walking
i felt free
looking up at God's sky
nothing wrong
i had suffered enough
it was all over
the utter misery
choking on my tears

i was miles away from anyone and anything
just one female human
nude with a flowing white dress over flesh
and the vast yellow field
the joy

i thought of my family
how great my mum and dad are
wonderful and complete characters, yes.
miraculously patient...
how dad saved my life
how i didn't want it saved
now i did, at last
and mum's endless selfless giving
her silent suffering
and dad's intense love
flowing out like a spring
how lucky i am
a vast fortune
the vast fortune their loves bring.

i am on the ground on my front in agony
a filthy stinking hand over my mouth
my dress pulled up
and stabbing pain inside my arse
again and again
then change the hole
i thought of Jesus.

no self pity
was the way to survive this. stop.
i thought of His suffering on the cross
my pain would go...
after some short time it did.

it went
he ran
a vagrant, i think
i looked around at where i was
called 999
i needed help
i needed to be tested
he couldn't be arrested
"no, i didn't see his face
i just want to know i am disease free
no, i won't need to talk to someone"
i just wanted to
be a daughter of Jesus
tell my mum
and get back to the picture i was painting of a sunflower
spunk and blood dripping down my thigh
my white dress far more violated than i
the vast yellow field
with a little red

i wondered how many other women
have my story to tell from in that field
i was so happy
i am no less ok now
i'll blot it out
it was impersonal
he didn't say a word
but for the predictable "bitch, slag, slut
you like it don't you"
i was thinking of st. Mary t'pinu
and it didn't reach me
vast beauty
vast love
if they say God's made up, then good.

they came to my aid.
i am disease free.
it happened.

i will walk there smiling again and soon
with someone perhaps
but it's all wrong and a disgrace
the mess we are in as a human race

i am smiling,
though it happened
one small scar on my right shoulder where i was pushed
there was a slice of stone in the field there
it looks like a stab wound.
it'll fade in time...

i was stabbed endlessly inside up
and into my most sacred zone
but nothing could lessen my purity
not even the oil seed rape

we're all walking wounded
i've been hurt far worse
than one quick burst
by a faceless stranger
fast physical pain
and vastly unimportant

just something that happened one day

the devil

gyp. in her pre-raphaelite hair
paler skin translucent aura
she looks like an angel there
but she's the devil: finer, sorer.

pool

i want to be alone in a pool
with just the glistening shimmering oil
that's water but
looks just the same
as it drains down our veins,
our skins natural butter

i want to look up and all i will see
is optical floaters and turquoise space.
i want to get my hair wet
so it weighs me down
and pulls my neck
and drip-drops chlorine between my cheeks
for the rest of the night
while i read and drink
in my wicker chair
that's seen a thousand
secrets,
filmic moments
just like this
oh, just like this

i want to float
not even swim
and feel the weightlessness of care
when it's seen for what it is
just as i see the mermaids there

they're evident
they're there all day
i talk to them
i just don't say

how we met

of all the castings
of all time...i
thank God daily
you chose mine...

i saw your beauty
starving, cold
you offered it
i took ahold

the wonder of your
mind, sublime
our eyes locked into
lovers' time

the atmosphere was
shallow, dull
so they could start the
singers' cull

saw money passed
from hand to hand.
she got the role
i got the man

and from that moment
we were one.
that show got cancelled
(which was fun)

mirror

if you look to see reflection
what you see is just a section
of the opposite of you.
mirrors madness. that is true.

dull or fresh

will you blow dust in my eyes and
slice my flesh up with your flint?
will your sun shine down on me then
ridicule me when i squint?

will you take me by the hair then
rape me in some car park close?
will you stop by, offer me
some words of praise for my new prose?

will you hurt my inside space, and
will you make them rub their hands?
will you take my only paintbrush
then draw hearts on sable sands?

will you publish all my love
then mop my vomit from the floor?
will you stick me in their faces...
maybe leave them wanting more?

will you make some tea and toast
or will you shove it in my mouth?
will you try to find me when i'm
hiding north-west-east of south?

will you set that lion free
and watch him savouring my flesh?
do you find my strangeness dull
or does it fire you up as fresh?

now roses bleed

you know how things fizzle out?
we never had that
too hot, too intense
too wonderful and perfect and energetic.
i loved you both so very much
why all my life had you not been there
when you were there
waiting sisters...

now roses bleed all over our knickers

oh girls, in general you are too, too wonderful!
if only one could marry you
with your lovely breasts and your deeper understanding

scream.

suddenly everything crashes around us
and everyone is decimated
dirt and dismay everywhere
like a lorry losing its load down a long highway
the stores are all out of cigarettes and wine
we had no escape but the disparity of words,
chanel lipstick and leotards
i close shut, cut off, and hide
to avoid things said
every single sigh
hid there hurting in my head.

i still shiver from a sneeze he did 8 months ago...
i live in fear.
i never pick up.
it's the highest insult to be ignored
they are right
but... what is my choice, girls, tell me that?
to hurt two sisters who'll got over it in weeks,
or be destroyed *forever* myself?
i know they suffer less. they told me so.
mine's an act of kindness here.
and i can say that before God on my knees.
surrounded by pink roses they adorn churches with here.
a perfect place to sing for Him.

a spiritual perfumery.

now roses bleed all over our knickers

ashes.
still smouldering, still on fire, more subtly tortured…
still burning gently up my thighs and into my hair
and right back round between me now
and oh how this agony reminds me of him
introducing pleasure to pain
and change my life
from suicide bids
to words, giggles, fun
and trust, that it's possible...
just jump!

ashes will still have me smarting.
they are still alive, they live!
little grey tributes to acute foregone agonies
they know
they knew
they gnaw at me there
want me to say it?
you want me to say it?
i'll do it then here:
they'll always love me for understanding.

now roses bleed all over our knickers

fools think they are grey and dead,
but they are quite alive instead
grey has life within it still,
i'm sure i've mentioned that before
never say you know for sure
you didn't know 'bout me at all
let's let it all exhausted lie
and kiss our love goodbye.

those memory cells will live on in me
a cleansing, confession, benediction
pain but pure beauty, it's not what you think.
they touched my anima, and i touched theirs

now roses bleed all over our knickers

fire cracker

saw you standing at the station
it's just lying, wearing blue
saw you thinking, saw that shadow
casting ash all over you

think you're such a fire cracker
such a gift to humankind
what you are is gift-wrapped ego.
big con to persuade the blind

getting in your taxi while
we wait for buses and more trains
what you wait for's never coming
we all get wet when it rains

then we see you fizzle, burn out
and we pray its not too late...
but you never warmed one soul, oh
you are stony. so's your fate.

fix it

you saw it, then took it and ripped it to bits
but you're not a junkie, a kid chasing hits
you put it all down to your being bear-wild
back on the stage, though, you're all meek and mild
so fix it. and act like the man that you seem…
don't worry. for millions. you'll still be the dream.

the journey

i thought about what could have been
the wind swept sand in my throat
my pace became more marked in time
the journey you sing on one note

i walked along the track bare feet
the wind swept sand in my eyes
i kept my path, always due north
the journey where everyone dies

a day

i've given a day all i could give it
tried, though restricted, so truly to live it
to fill it full up and to drink from the cup
and it's too late to be anxious with it

prince

smooth grey
long stretches
curled ball
autistic sketches
you remember
from september
to december in
...atoms.

how many
left to right
from left to right
to left then right
you print it in your head
you prince
stamp it in there
charcoal, terracotta
press the numbers
press them harder
harder still
your tick is charming

get some vapid
network host
and reproduce it
on a sparkly tv show...

and we all see you needle wince
cos you forgot
one dot

i worship talent
i revere
everything you are.
i'm near.

to lunch with you
would be a thrill
in awe of you.
i take my pill
to stop myself from getting more
like you, whom i do so adore.

rocker

there once was a hard heavy rocker
whose personal life was a shocker
she danced in barbed wire
right in front of his fire
stiletto shoved right up his cocker

water at stintino

when you shall see it, i shall too
below, above
i'm seeing blue
it just reflects my darling love

and into words
you put your thoughts
and into birds
all coloured sorts

i will put mine
or in sea brine
i'll pour my fears
instead of tears

and you can taste well
when you eat
and i can smell
beneath the heat

and minuscule
the atoms clear
as water
at stintino here

i don't know
what i want to say
except i love you
all the way

afterlife

and so soft things now come to me
like white foam bobbing on the sea
i hear the shore, the tide's refrain
"i go in then go out again"

i smell the sea salt giving light
to other senses in the night
i smell my loved one's body living
feel his breath, the taking, giving
touch his skin so soft so young
as if it's time had just begun

i see the rise and fall of dust
we know the rule, it truly must
be rhythmic in its actions here
as all of earth has to be near
to something similar, and as
each speck we have the gravitas
to be or not to be as one.

the afterlife has now begun

index of titles